FELLOW TEAMBUILDERS ENDORSE
The Team That Jesus Built

"Janet Thompson has a heart for the Lord and a heart for raising up women who have a heart for Him. She has given us many tools to mentor women and to grow together as women. As a leader herself, she has developed effective and multiplying teams. Her chapter in *Transformed Lives* by the same name as this book has helped many women's leaders grow their own teams. Thank you, Janet, for expanding on 'The Team That Jesus Built' as we continue to model His leadership through our teams."
—Chris Adams, senior lead women's ministry specialist, LifeWay Christian Resources

"In *The Team That Jesus Built*, Janet Thompson offers practical, step-by-step advice for building, remodeling, or rejuvenating a ministry team. Although specifically written from the perspective of women's ministry, *The Team That Jesus Built* equally applies to every kind of ministry leadership team. Every leader will benefit from Janet's experience and wisdom gained from years following Jesus in the trenches of ministry."
—Kathy Howard, minister of adult education at Fannin Terrace Baptist Church and author of *Before His Throne, God's Truth Revealed*, and *Unshakeable Faith*

the Team *that* Jesus Built

New Hope® Publishers
P. O. Box 12065
Birmingham, AL 35202-2065
www.newhopepublishers.com
New Hope Publishers is a division of WMU®

Library of Congress Cataloging-in-Publication Data

Thompson, Janet, 1947-
  The team that Jesus built : how to develop, equip, and commission a women's
ministry team / Janet Thompson.
     p. cm.
  ISBN-13: 978-1-59669-300-5
  ISBN-10: 1-59669-300-2
  1. Women in church work. I. Title.
  BV4415.T56 2011
  253.082--dc22

                      2010053989

Interior design by Michel Lê

ISBN-10: 1-59669-300-2
ISBN-13: 978-1-59669-300-5

N114135• 0311 • 3M1

the Team that
Jesus Built

How to
Develop,
Equip, and
Commission
a Women's
Ministry
Team

Janet Thompson

NEW HOPE
PUBLISHERS
Birmingham, Alabama

Other New Hope books by

Janet Thompson

"Face-to-Face" M&M Mentoring Bible study series

Face-to-Face with Naomi and Ruth: Together for the Journey

Face-to-Face with Mary and Martha: Sisters in Christ

Face-to-Face with Euodia and Syntyche: From Conflict to Community

Face-to-Face with Elizabeth and Mary: Generation to Generation

Face-to-Face with Priscilla and Aquila: Balancing Life and Ministry

To

*Women's ministry visionary directors who selflessly serve
the women in your church*

and

The teams that faithfully serve with you

Contents

Section Three: Maturing, Equipping, and Commissioning the Team

The Team That Jesus Built

Jesus . . . as the builder of a house has greater honor than the house itself.
For every house is built by someone, but God is the builder of everything.

—HEBREWS 3:3–4

Every year, the Saddleback Church Woman to Woman Mentoring Ministry Administrative Team went on a weekend planning retreat. We would find a cabin in the mountains or a condominium at the beach or in the desert, and settle in for a time of fun, calendar planning, vision casting, training, and relaxation (although the team would laugh at that last word, since I usually planned a full schedule!).

Months prior to a retreat, I prayed for the Lord to give me a theme and a Scripture. Early in the ministry while praying about a retreat theme, the Lord surprised me with an old children's nursery rhyme, "The House That Jack Built." When I told one of our team members that the Lord had put this cumulative jingle in my mind, she said she had it in a children's picture book. Here are several stanzas, to give you an idea of how the cadence builds:

The House That Jack Built (Nursery Rhyme)

Author: Randolph Caldecott

> This is the House that Jack built.
> This is the Rat
> That ate the malt
> That lay in the House that Jack built.
>
> This is the Cat,
> That killed the Rat,
> That ate the malt
> That lay in the House that Jack built.
>
> This is the Dog,
> That worried the Cat,
> That killed the Rat,
> That ate the malt
> That lay in the House that Jack built.
>
> This is the Cow with the crumpled horn,
> That tossed the Dog,
> That worried the Cat,
> That killed the Rat,
> That ate the malt
> That lay in the House that Jack built.

You're probably laughing as I did, because there is nothing particularly spiritual about this poem. After many questioning prayers, I realized God wanted me to rewrite the jingle as "The Team That Jesus Built," which became the theme for our retreat that year.

The heart of my poem, "The Team That Jesus Built," is that every woman's initiation into ministry service starts with attending church and discovering an opportunity to become involved. Initially, she helps in small ways, and then she may serve on a team requiring more time and responsibility. Apprenticeship and leadership roles are the next progression, and ultimately, she becomes a shepherd coach on the administrative team.

THE TEAM THAT JESUS BUILT

This is the Shepherd Coach
That joined the Team
That Jesus built

This is the Apprentice
That assisted the Shepherd Coach
That joined the Team
That Jesus built

This is the Team Leader
That became the Apprentice
That assisted the Shepherd Coach
That joined the Team
That Jesus built

This is the Team
That followed the Team Leader
That became the Apprentice
That assisted the Shepherd Coach
That joined the Team
That Jesus built

This is the Helper who said, "Use me,"
That came on the Team
That followed the Team Leader
That became the Apprentice
That assisted the Shepherd Coach
That joined the Team
That Jesus built

This is the M&M who went to a Coffee
That was the Helper who said, "Use me,"
That came on the Team
That followed the Team Leader
That became the Apprentice

That assisted the Shepherd Coach
That joined the Team
That Jesus built

This is the woman, a Saddleback attendee,
That turned into the M&M who went to a Coffee
That was the Helper who said, "Use me,"
That came on the Team
That followed the Team Leader
That became the Apprentice
That assisted the Shepherd Coach
That joined the Team
That Jesus built

This is the bulletin notice and Fellowship Table Lady
That welcomed the woman, a Saddleback attendee,
That turned into the M&M who went to a Coffee
That was the Helper who said, "Use me,"
That came on the Team
That followed the Team Leader
That became the Apprentice
That assisted the Shepherd Coach
That joined the team
That Jesus built

This is your neighbor you invited on Sunday
That saw the bulletin notice and Fellowship Table Lady
That welcomed the woman, a Saddleback attendee,
That turned into the M&M who went to a Coffee
That was the Helper who said, "Use me,"
That came on the Team
That followed the Team Leader
That became the Apprentice
That assisted the Shepherd Coach
That joined the team
That Jesus built

We were at a cabin in the mountains for "The Team That Jesus Built" retreat. During one of our breaks, the team took a walk around the neighborhood and returned insisting I go with them to see something. They took me to the next street and showed me a cabin with a sign in front that read, "The House That Jack Built"! My shrieks of delight and amazement echoed throughout the mountains. The team and I knew God was confirming that I had heard Him correctly, and He wanted us to work on team building "Jesus-style" that year.

The verse God gave me to go with our team-building retreat theme was the opening verse of this chapter, Hebrews 3:3–4. Jesus, not the leader, is the builder of the team. A leader is only as good as her dependence on the Lord.

Our team goal became learning how to construct *The Team That Jesus Built*. This book passes on to you the many lessons we learned in the building process. Jesus built His team and left us scriptural blueprints for building, maturing, equipping, and commissioning our own teams. I pray *The Team That Jesus Built* provides you with tools, guidance, and encouragement whether you're building a new team or remodeling or refurbishing an existing team.

Note: For more on team retreats see chapter 22, "Jesus Retreated with His Team."

Acknowledgments

Ministries need teams, and I've been blessed to work with teams of women dedicated to serving Jesus and working on His team with me. I thank God for those women. I wouldn't be writing this book without their support and dedication to building teams Jesus-style.

Authors need the support and prayers of The Team That Jesus Built. Only Jesus could put together such a winning team for me.

Our family team is built on the firm foundation of Jesus Christ. My husband, Dave, our four children and their spouses, and our incredibly fun and precious 11 grandchildren are my cheerleaders and encouragers. I love and cherish each one of you.

I partner with a godly publishing and marketing team at New Hope Publishers. Thank you for sharing my vision and making it look so good!

On my About His Work Ministries team, I'm fortunate to have my literary agent, Steve Laube. Bless you, Steve, for effortlessly and conscientiously taking care of the business side of my writing.

Friends are essential to every life team and Linda, Susan, and Sharron, you keep me balanced and healthy with our morning walks. Thank you for rides to the airport, prayers, encouragement, and inspiration. Sharron, the time and energy you devote to helping edit my manuscripts is invaluable. Words cannot convey my appreciation. You are friends who love at all times.

People need the Lord. Thank You, Jesus, for teaching me how to build teams that help share that message.

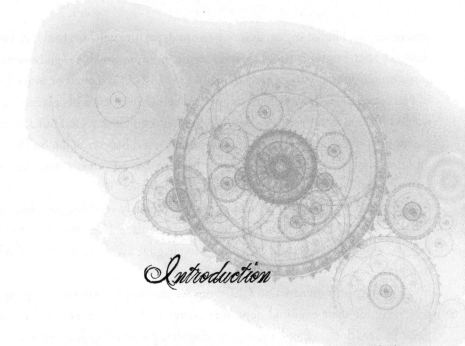

Introduction

Churches need leaders who have the skills to equip others to team with them in ministry.
                                          —C. GENE WILKES

Ministry leaders need to ask themselves, "When is it time to give away the ministry?"

I toss this question out to the audience during leadership training sessions. It's also the title of the chapter on building an administrative team in my book *Woman to Woman Mentoring Ministry Coordinator's Guide.* I often receive these answers:

- When you lose your passion.
- When God calls you somewhere else.
- When you're no longer effective.
- When the ministry becomes too big for you to handle on your own.
- When you're burned out!

All negative responses—did you notice? With a capable, well-trained team sharing the load, you won't lose your passion, become ineffective or overwhelmed, or burned out. And I don't believe God ever calls us out of an area of serving Him in any capacity when our departure will hurt the work being done for Him, but we can and should recruit and train capable replacements to carry on our work. Throughout the Bible, when God removed or moved one of His leaders, He always had an apprentice ready to take his place. Moses trained Joshua as his replacement. Elijah mentored Elisha. God put David in position to take King Saul's place. David mentored his son Solomon to carry on after him. When God called Jesus back to heaven, Jesus left a team of trained disciples ready to carry on His earthly work.

Jesus planned for His departure by systematically selecting, building, and training a team. He groomed the disciples to replace Him from the day He called them into service, and He progressively gave away His earthly ministry to them.

Wise business owners and CEOs ensure the longevity of the company by preparing for their eventual departure. After building a successful business, these leaders don't want the company dissolving when they leave or retire, so they continuously and systematically groom others to replace them. When Bill Gates, the founder and head of Microsoft, stepped down from the company's day-to-day operations to devote time to his wife's and his philanthropic foundation, he issued a press statement that this was not a sudden decision and that he would remain involved with the company. Gates didn't announce one specific person replacing him at the top—perhaps he had teams in place ready to carry on his work.

Bill Gates and Microsoft had become synonymous. Gates built the company, but wisely ascertained it was time to let those whom he had groomed step into his shoes. Gates didn't abandon the company, close it down, get tired of it, or lose his passion; he simply knew the company couldn't outlive him if its survival depended on him.

I once observed a very successful and life-changing men's ministry dissolve after only three years when the founder and leader left to serve in another area. He was the glue that kept the ministry together and when he moved on, the ministry folded because there wasn't a trained apprentice or team sharing his vision and ready to continue in his absence.

My heart breaks when I hear stories of a ministry ending because the leader became ill, moved, went to serve in another ministry, started a new job, or for whatever reason, left and didn't groom a capable person or team to take his or her place.

Sadly, these scenarios occur repeatedly in the church. Often the founder of a ministry is a passionate visionary with great ideas, but she doesn't develop an apprentice or administrative team to carry on her vision or help develop the ministry. Most churches have a list of ministries that started with a bang and then fizzled—not for lack of people needing the benefits of the ministry, but often because the leader left without having an equipped team in place.

When is it time to give away the ministry? Answer: The moment you begin developing a team. That's right. Just like Jesus, you continuously seek and train qualified women to whom you can delegate and multiply your efforts. You probably don't want to do women's ministry all by yourself; most people will let you, however, unless you ask for and utilize their help. Jesus left us a model to follow and emulate as leaders, team builders, and team members. Let's explore that model together.

SECTION ONE:

Why Lead Like Jesus?

~ CHAPTER 1 ~

My Story

Jesus said, "Feed my sheep." — JOHN 21:17

My journey into ministry had the mark of God's hand from the beginning, as I'm sure yours did as well. Some of us recognize God as the "still small voice" and the "door opener," and others of us wake up one morning, discover we're in ministry, and wonder how we got there!

When I received "the call" from the Lord, I was attending Saddleback Church in Lake Forest, California. At the time, I was running an insurance agency and working on a Master of Arts in Christian Leadership, focusing on Ministry of the Laity, at Fuller Theological Seminary, which I thought would be a nice complement to my master of business administration.

One year into seminary, I began questioning what God's plans were for me. I decided to attend a Multnomah Bible College and Seminary "Women in Ministry" leadership conference in Portland, Oregon, with the express purpose of researching opportunities available to women besides directing a women's ministry in a church. My intent was to convince God and myself that women's ministry was not my call. Business was my forte and where I wanted to serve.

The Lord did speak clearly to me at that conference, but not in the manner I expected. While drinking my after-dinner coffee one night I heard, "Go and Feed my sheep." I peered over my coffee cup to see who was talking to me about sheep, but no one was speaking to me. I thought: *What sheep? Where? And what will I feed them when I find them?* The voice came back again more emphatic than before, "Feed My sheep." I muttered under my breath an obedient, "OK." The rest of the evening, I wondered what this meant, and what I had just agreed to do!

Calling my husband later that night, I told him I thought the Lord spoke to me. We prayed the Holy Spirit would give me the meaning of "Feed My sheep." The Lord was quick and gracious to respond to our prayers. The next morning, I arrived at the opening session eager for another day of learning. As I settled into my chair, the speaker announced she would be speaking from the "Familiar Scriptures in John 21:15–17 where Jesus asks Peter three times if Peter loves Him. Three times Peter responds, 'Yes, Lord, You know I love You.' Three times Jesus instructs Peter, 'Feed my sheep.'"

Glancing at the agenda for the day, I let out a startled, "Wow!" The morning's topic was "Shepherding Women in Your Church." I sensed the Holy Spirit's nudging and realized the Lord was answering my prayer. I felt God had the wrong woman—but I had said yes to Him, so whether I liked it or not, it seemed women were the sheep and in some way I was going to feed them spiritually.

Within several weeks of arriving home, two women asked me to mentor them. One was from my insurance business and the other a young friend of one of my daughters. I thought of the times in my life when I wished someone had been there to mentor me, all the mistakes I might have avoided if someone had cared enough to give me wise counsel and advice from a Christian perspective and kept me accountable to walking with the Lord.

As I mentored these two women, God created a series of events confirming that *feeding* meant mentoring and the *sheep* were women. I began wondering if the Lord had a plan for me that went beyond being a mentor. There probably were herds of "sheep" needing to be fed, and I couldn't mentor them all on my own. I sensed the Lord wanted me to use my mentoring experience with these two women and my leadership training from the business world to encourage and teach other women how to be mentors. Could He be telling me to start a mentoring ministry?

When visions of a mentoring ministry started taking shape and ideas came to mind of how to start one, I began the process of launching the Woman to Woman Mentoring Ministry at Saddleback Church. In spite of my lack of confidence and no previous experience in leading or serving on a women's ministry team at church, the Lord blessed this mentoring ministry.

When I started Woman to Woman Mentoring, my mission was to create a ministry that would outlive me and not center on one person, so my title became "ministry visionary director." I would develop and direct the ministry, while training and mentoring a team prepared to carry on in my absence.

Six years after launching the ministry, I was diagnosed with breast cancer requiring surgery and subsequent radiation therapy. The ministry never missed a beat because we had in place The Team That Jesus Built, and the team members took ownership of their respective areas of the ministry. The team stepped up to the plate and the ministry work continued during my illness. When I recovered, we all realized the value of my having systematically and progressively given away the ministry to them.

Equally important was that, after giving away the ministry, I didn't take it back. When I recovered, I let the capable team members carry on leading the ministry, while I became a consultant "visionary" helping fine-tune their respective areas. The team learned what I had been telling them all along— they really could do it without me. That should be every leader's ultimate goal. Even if you stay on as the ministry visionary director until your homecoming with Jesus, a well-trained, equipped, and capable team helps you avoid:

- Losing your passion.
- Becoming overwhelmed.
- Wanting to leave.
- Becoming ineffective.
- Leaving a void in your absence.

I was asked if I felt sad watching the team function so well without me. Was there a sense of loss? Absolutely not! I was overjoyed. I was grateful that what I had worked for, prayed for, and taught to others was coming to fruition: a fulfillment of my belief that no ministry should ever be about one person.

My title remained Visionary, and I could fulfill that role by globally sharing what Jesus has taught me with other ministries and churches.

In this book, I'll mentor you from my team-building experiences. I don't claim to have team building figured out; like you, I'm continually learning. As with our faith, growing in leadership is a lifetime process.

People may become leaders by responding in a healthy manner to all they encounter in life, but they will not become spiritual leaders unless God calls them to this role and equips them for it. Secular leadership is something to which people can aspire. It can be achieved through sheer force of will. Spiritual leadership, on the other hand, is not a role for which one applies. Rather, it is assigned by God. God determines each person's assignment. Historically, God has chosen ordinary people, most of whom were not looking for a divine assignment. Nevertheless, God saw something in their hearts that led him to assign particular tasks.

—HENRY AND RICHARD BLACKABY, *Spiritual Leadership*

~ CHAPTER 2 ~

You Are the Designated Leader —But Is Anyone Following?

"Follow Me!" So, leaving everything behind, he got up and began to follow Him.
                                        —LUKE 5:27–28 (HCSB)

Jesus Had Followers

Jesus knew how to attract followers. With a simple command, *"Follow Me,"* men who had no intention of ever being evangelists or going into ministry left everything behind and followed Jesus. It wasn't long before many men and women were following Him everywhere He went. People wanted to be in His presence and they wanted to serve in His ministry.

What Kind of a Leader Are You?

Some women are born to lead. As little girls playing house they insisted on being the mother, or when playing school they had to be the schoolteacher. They picked the games to play with their friends and led the way on trikes, bikes, hikes, or skates. In high school, they tried out for *head* cheerleader— not just cheerleader. Or class *president*—not vice-president. Thriving in the limelight, they were comfortable at the head of the class, on stage, or speaking in public. These "born leaders" usually choose jobs or life roles that keep them leading someone or something.

The above description describes me: I was a bossy little girl. While I could capture or demand the prize role of mother or schoolteacher and convince my little pals to play my choice of games, I wanted them to play by *my* rules. As you can imagine, it wasn't long before my friends drifted away and I was playing by myself!

As a leader, I used to struggle with thinking I could do things better and easier myself. Who needs a team who might mess things up or take too long to get things done? (Are you tracking with me?) I recently heard a sermon pointing out that pride is at the root of: "I can do it better and faster than anyone else." In fact, pride is at the heart of: bossy, insecure, feeling inadequate, feeling too adequate.

The true sign of a leader is whether she has followers. I once heard a woman announce she was a leader, and I knew immediately she wasn't because a leader doesn't have to tell you she's a leader. You know a leader by the group of people willing to follow her.

Maybe the "typical" leader profile doesn't fit you. Instead, you wonder why you ever agreed to take on a leadership position. You hate being out in front, are terrified of public speaking, and would rather serve on the team than lead it. Still, you find yourself in charge and, like Moses, you're fearfully telling God you can't lead. In his book, *Leading from the Heart*, Michael Mack says, "When you say you have no gifts or abilities, you're saying more about God than about yourself; you're saying that God hasn't gifted you." What you're really implying is that God can't lead through you, when in faith you know He can. Where God guides, God provides.

You're not in your current leadership position by accident. You may feel unqualified and incapable, and on your own strength, you are. We all are. But you can do all things through Christ who strengthens you (Philippians 4:13). You can do this, and soon you will be helping others see they can do it too. Even with your misgivings, exude confidence and a desire to lead or you too might have no one following.

So how can you become a godly leader with the right motivation and confidence? At the risk of sounding bossy, *"Follow my example, as I follow the example of Christ"* (1 Corinthians 11:1).

The Way Not to Develop a Team

In the *Woman to Woman Mentoring Ministry Coordinator's Guide*, I tell my story of making radical mistakes and learning important lessons when first developing an administrative team.

When the Lord led me to start Woman to Woman Mentoring, it soared right from the beginning. Everyone, including me, was grateful that I had taken the initiative to start the ministry without waiting to develop a team. However, at the end of the first year, I realized the ministry was outgrowing me. I put out a plea for administrative help and received seven offers of assistance. I was ecstatic and marveled that people were willing to serve without pay. I decided to call the members of the administrative team shepherd coaches, nurturing leaders.

Saddleback Church has a class called 301 in which members discover how to use their God-given gifts for serving the church. At Saddleback, we call it your SHAPE (spiritual gifts, heart, abilities, personality, experiences). People work best when utilizing their natural gifts and talents, and I thought the women who had offered to help administratively would know their own SHAPE and qualifications. So I let them choose where they wanted to serve. When one woman offered to serve as financial shepherd coach, another woman confirmed that this was a perfect area for her because she kept her checkbook balanced to the penny. She knew her SHAPE! The women left our first team meeting ready to take on their new administrative tasks. I breathed a sigh of relief. The ministry would soon be able to get along without me.

Well, maybe not yet.

By the next administrative team meeting, we had grown from 7 to 12 shepherd coaches. I thought that was a prophetic number and hoped it would signify the plans the Lord had for us. I even wrote a ministry newsletter article about having 12 disciples just like Jesus. It wasn't long before I learned the error of my ways. The only resemblance to Jesus' example and the way I went about developing a team—we both ended up with 12!

I quickly learned that if the administrative team is too big, it easily becomes a committee bogged down with numerous opinions, personalities, and conflicts. Yes, conflicts even among Christians! I hadn't explored the spiritual maturity of any of the shepherd coaches or their motivation for serving on the team. I didn't check their heart to see if they wanted to *follow* me or *compete* with me. Did they have the passion for serving that I did? Were they willing to make this position their focused ministry? Had their spouses agreed? So many unasked questions came back to haunt me.

Soon, it became evident that several team members had their own agenda. They weren't interested in working as a team but only wanted their ideas heard. It was a time of turmoil and the lack of support was overwhelming. I realized my mistakes as I watched the Lord whittle down the team of 12 to 3 shepherd coaches and me, and then I sought guidance.

I prayed to learn from this experience. I longed to lead like Jesus. *The Team That Jesus Built* is my humble attempt at passing on to you what I learned. I pray the team-building principles of Jesus revolutionize the way you do ministry, as they did for me. The transition of the team *increasing* and me *decreasing* is what I hope to share with you in the remainder of this book. Let me tell you how my little team of three and I regrouped and followed Jesus to become The Team That Jesus Built!

How I Learned to Lead Like Jesus And You Can Too!

The distinguishing characteristic of leaders is that they use their experience as learning tools and they gain renewed motivation from their failures.

— RICHARD AND HENRY BLACKABY

My way of forming a team had failed, but I knew it wasn't the end. The ministry was going well, in spite of me. My goal was to determine what I had done wrong in building a team, correct it, and continue growing and learning as a leader. You may be in one of the following situations:

~ Starting a ministry and building a team.

~ Remodeling the remnants of a team, starting over with a new team, or inheriting a team from a predecessor.

~ Looking for ways to refurbish and rejuvenate an existing team and take it to the next level of leadership.

Whatever your reasons for picking up this book, God wants you to succeed. You're not in this leadership position by accident. It's OK temporarily to indulge thoughts of:

~ I failed.

~ I made a mistake.

~ I need to start over.

- I don't know what I'm doing.
- I feel inadequate.
- I'm not a leader.

Those are common first reactions to a ministry problem, but don't believe them or let your misgivings be an excuse for not learning to lead in the position where God has put you. Satan will do everything he can to discourage you. Maybe you even hesitated reading this book because you're not sure you want to succeed. Wouldn't it be easier to give up and move on? Probably, but is it the best thing for the women of your church? Is it what God wants you to do?

Whatever type of ministry or team you lead, and whatever the size of your church, the principles I share in this book will work with prayer, effort, and energy. Why can I make such a bold statement? Because I'm offering principles based on how Jesus led His team. He didn't have Harvard graduates to work with or men highly skilled in leading and managing. In fact, His team members were probably less qualified than those on your team, yet Jesus turned over the spiritual future of the world to them! Here is a cute story that puts it all into perspective:

> A consultant team once evaluated some of Jesus' disciples:
> Simon Peter is emotionally unstable and given to fits of temper.
> Andrew has absolutely no leadership qualities.
> The sons of Zebedee, James and John, place personal interests above company loyalty.
> Thomas demonstrates a questioning attitude that would tend to undermine morale.
> We feel that it is our duty to tell You that Matthew has been blacklisted by the Greater Jerusalem Better Business Bureau.
> James, the son of Alphaeus, and Thaddaeus definitely have radical leanings, and they both registered a high score on the manic-depressive scale.
> One of the candidates, however, shows great potential. He is a man of ability and resourcefulness. . . . We recommend Judas Iscariot as Your comptroller and right-hand man.
>
> —*The Baptist Messenger*, SEPTEMBER 27, 1984

Jesus let me fail at building my first team because He wanted me to come to Him for direction and guidance. I went into the position of ministry visionary director with scholastic credentials for leading, but I fell flat on my face. There was nothing wrong with what I learned in school, but I still had the world's perspective on leading and Jesus wanted me to lead *His* way. What was that way? That became my quest. I hope it's yours also.

How to Use The Team That Jesus Built

The format of this book follows the building theme of Hebrews 3:3–4.

- *Title of the chapter*
- *Topic Scripture*
- *The Cornerstone* — Jesus' foundational leadership principle
- *The Blueprint* — Brief discussion of the leadership principle
- *Customize* — Specific ways to modify the principle to apply to your current circumstance and stage of leadership
- Building: creating a new team
- Remodeling: rebuilding a struggling, unproductive, or inherited team
- Refurbishing: maturing and rejuvenating an established team and helping team members build their own teams
- *Tools* — Recommended resources, suggestions, and reproducible forms
- *Team-Building Project* — An application or exercise to illustrate the principle
- *Leader to Leader* — My experience with the leadership principle and suggestions for your implementation
- *Finishing Touches* — Final tips and suggestions
- *Mentoring Moment* — Encouragement

This book addresses women's ministry directors, but the principles apply to all stages and levels of leadership and team building and all sizes of teams. You may be in a small church and feel like you're doing everything yourself, because you probably are. This book will give you tools to help share the joys of serving with the other women in your church. Just start out doing everything discussed on a smaller scale, and watch your team grow.

- In the "Leader to Leader" section, I am writing to the women's ministry director, who I am calling the women's ministry *visionary* director, and shortening to ministry visionary director. All levels of leadership within the ministry will benefit from the discussion.
- When I refer to "the team," it's the ministry visionary director's administrative team comprised of *shepherd coaches*. The title shepherd coach implies loving and nurturing while directing and guiding.
- The Book of Mark in the Bible is the scriptural premise for *The Team That Jesus Built*. You might want to stop now and read Mark.
- Don't implement everything at once. Take time to work your way through this book slowly, incorporating the new ideas and concepts and giving each one time to develop and become routine before moving on to the next step. There's no rush; change is a process.

If you picked up this book as the leader, director, minister, or pastor of a ministry, I encourage you to share the book with all the team leaders in the ministry so they can use it in developing their teams. If you are a team leader in a ministry, but not the ministry director, this book is for you too. Apply *The Team That Jesus Built* to your team, and then share it with your ministry director.

Time to Start Construction

I wasn't discouraged when the team crumbled around me. I felt sad, disappointed, frustrated, but not hopeless. I knew I was doing something wrong and needed to learn the right way from the Master Team Builder, Jesus: a Leader with an unlikely team that changed history. I wanted to delve into and apply the only way I knew would work—Jesus' leadership style.

The first principle I learned in developing a team was that Jesus was tempted.

SECTION TWO:

Building the Team

~ CHAPTER 4 ~

Jesus Was Tempted

Jesus, full of the Holy Spirit, returned from the Jordan and was led by the
Spirit in the desert, where for forty days he was tempted by the devil.

—LUKE 4:1–2

The Cornerstone

Luke 4:1–5 tells us that between the time of being baptized in the Spirit and starting His public ministry, Jesus was tempted by Satan with *"the cravings of sinful man, the lust of his eyes, and the boasting of what he has and does"* (1 John 2:16).

With each temptation, Jesus made a choice and took a stand (Luke 4:3–12). Without hesitation, His response was a firm, "No!" supported by Scripture. Satan retreated, for the moment, *"When the devil had finished all this tempting, he left him until an opportune time"* (v. 13).

The Blueprint

In *Strength in Servant Leadership*, Paul A. Cedar discusses an inevitable temptation of every leader: "One of the temptations leaders face is to build our own personal kingdom; to control our own loyal following; to look upon the flock that God has entrusted to our care as our own. We develop a vocabulary that includes such possessive phrases as 'my congregation' or 'my people.'"

Satan tried to entice Jesus with the same temptations he uses to lure today's leaders, and pride is at the center of each one (Luke 4:3–12):

- Self sufficiency—hungering for success, popularity, recognition, possessions, and wealth (v. 3).
- Greed—lusting after what isn't or shouldn't be ours (vv. 5–7).
- Power—retaining all authority, splendor, and fame for ourselves; doing something foolish and expecting God to rescue us (vv. 9–11).

If Satan tempted Jesus, He *will* tempt us. Take precautions to guard your heart and your mind from falling prey to Satan's sly and cunning ways (1 Peter 5:6–11).

Customize

BUILDING: As you build the ministry and team, surround yourself with godly people who keep you accountable. Ask them to listen for you referring to *my* ministry or *my* team so that you can correct ownership (in your mind and in your speaking) to whom this ministry *really* belongs—Jesus.

REMODELING: Prayerfully review the temptation list in the "Team-Building Project" below. Could any of these be the nucleus of ministry or team problems? Acknowledgment is the first step toward overcoming and conquering temptations that could lead to sin and possibly destroy your remodeling efforts.

REFURBISHING: Establish accountability partners within the team to alert each other when they see pride or temptations infiltrating their service.

Tools

Every morning pray through the armor of God in Ephesians 6:10–18 for spiritual protection against Satan. Use the following analogy to help you pray.

Roman Soldier   Spiritual Analogy

1. BELT OF TRUTH (V. 14A)

Put belt on first to cinch in a loose robe or toga
Held sheath for sword
Breastplate attached to it

Truth central to Christianity

2. BREASTPLATE OF RIGHTEOUSNESS (V. 14B)

Protected heart and lungs

Maintain pure heart and emotion

3. SANDALS OR SHOES OF THE GOSPEL OF PEACE (V. 15)

Studs or nails on soles for a firm foundation
No slipping or sliding into temptation
On an incline could hold his ground
Protection from sharpened sticks implanted in the ground, sticking up at an angle

Prevent backsliding and slipping

Ready to share the gospel
Progress spiritually

4. SHIELD OF FAITH (V. 16)

Wood with protective metal coating, or leather soaked in water to extinguish fiery arrows
Repelled flaming arrows that might lodge in it

Protection against Satan's lies

5. HELMET OF SALVATION (V. 17A)

Made of leather embedded with pieces of metal
Designed to withstand a crushing blow to the head

Guard brain, mind, thoughts

Remember you're saved!

6. SWORD OF THE SPIRIT (V. 17B)

Only offensive weapon

Word of God/Scripture

Team-Building Project

Give an accountability partner permission to tell you if she or he sees you giving in to any of the following temptations or sins. As you read through the list, ask God to reveal to your heart any areas where you're tempted.

___ Making all the decisions yourself

___ Reveling in the limelight

___ Seeking the praises of others

___ Doing everything yourself

___ Being controlling and inflexible

___ Demanding perfection

___ Acting foolishly

___ Showing impatience

___ Being lustful

___ Being argumentative

___ Reacting in anger

___ Misplacing ambition

___ Disrespecting or rejecting authority

___ Going against church policy

___ Focusing more on your own good than the good of the ministry

___ Not developing a capable team to assist you

___ Neglecting to develop the next generation of leaders

___ Refusing to seek an apprentice

___ Deriving self-esteem from the ministry position

___ Building an unapproachable wall around yourself

___ Creating a clique or "in crowd" atmosphere

___ Exaggerating

___ Bending the rules

___ Lying

___ Being greedy

___ Fill in your personal temptations if not listed above:

_____

_____

Review the above list of potential temptations with the team and discuss answers to the following questions.

What steps are you taking to avoid temptation?

1. _____
2. _____
3. _____
4. _____

What is your strategy for defeating temptation?
1. _____
2. _____
3. _____
4. _____

List the names of those to enlist as accountability partners.
1. _____
2. _____
3. _____

Compose a kind and loving response when you receive praise for the ministry work you are doing. Let your words be a testimony that with God's direction, the other person also could become a vessel used by God.

Leader to Leader

Everyone at church was congratulating me on the success of the mentoring ministry and exclaiming over the testimonies of lives changing. It was tempting to take the credit and kudos and pat myself on the back for what a great job I was doing.

I enlisted my husband and a friend as accountability partners to help me guard against the temptation of pride. I gave them permission to point out to me privately and lovingly if they heard me referring to the ministry as "my" ministry without giving the Lord credit, or if they saw me acting boastful. It wasn't long before sharing the wondrous works of the Lord replaced self-focused words and actions.

I knew the success of the ministry was not about me—it was about God working in and through me. I was simply the willing vessel who said yes to the Lord. As I learned to convey that message, the temptation of claiming ownership of the ministry vanished. However, daily I had to guard against its return or other potential temptations. Satan will use anything to trip up the amazing work God does through our ministries.

Satan tempts every leader and the more successful and influential the ministry, the more Satan tries to topple it. Beware. Keep your guard up. I literally pray the armor of God in Ephesians 6:10–18 every morning. I also developed kind responses to accolades from good-hearted well-wishers and encouragers. Feel free to use them.

- "The Lord's ministry is going great. It feels good knowing I'm in His will."
- "Oh, I can't take the credit. God is doing amazing things in the ministry. Please pray for His continued blessings."
- "Thank you for your kind words. The praise and glory goes to the Lord. It's *His* ministry, which He has blessed with many serving hearts. I love serving with Him and with them."

Pride fools us into thinking we couldn't be tempted or we can resist temptation on our own—and that sets us up for failure. God hates pride (Proverbs 8:13). Yet, pride is at the center of almost everything we do unless we recognize and fight it the same way Jesus did—by knowing God's Word and hiding it in our hearts so that we won't sin against Him (Psalm 119:11). If you want to stay humble and avoid temptation, make the Bible your *"bread of life"* (John 6:35). You wouldn't go a day without eating unless you were sick or fasting. If you go a day without the Lord's Word, you'll be sick in heart and empty in spirit.

Finishing Touches

- It's OK to be proud of the ministry and the team's work, but give credit where credit is due — Jesus.

- Did any of the temptations discussed in this chapter resonate with you, or are you thinking: *I really don't think I have a problem with any of these?* If that's your response, then let someone close to you look at the list and grant that person permission to point out what she or he sees. Often, we're unaware of our own faults. To establish an accountability agreement with someone:

1. Delineate the areas where you want accountability.
2. Inform your accountability partner how and when you want to be held accountable.
3. Formally permit your accountability partner to keep you accountable.
4. Don't avoid the person, or he or she may get discouraged and quit trying to help you.
5. Pray about the areas identified by your accountability partner.

- The Spirit led Jesus into the wilderness of temptation. God may allow you to face potentially tempting situations or wilderness times to grow your character, purify your motives, and solidify your calling to lead. It's part of leadership preparation.

Mentoring Moment

Leaders don't need to look for temptation; temptation finds them.

Jesus Started His Ministry, Then Developed a Team

Jesus returned to Galilee in the power of the Spirit, and news about him
spread through the whole countryside. He taught in their synagogues, and
everyone praised him.
— LUKE 4:14–15

The Cornerstone

Jesus didn't wait until He had a team together before launching into His God-given call of public ministry. Prior to recruiting the first disciples, Jesus started His ministry by driving out evil spirits, teaching, and healing (Luke 4:14–44).

The Blueprint

A ministry can start with the Lord and you. Traditionally, teams develop *before* starting a ministry, but with the untraditional method, a team develops *from within* the ministry. You observe future team members serving *before* inviting them to join the team. Start the ministry and the team will come. Family members or friends can help you launch the ministry, while the administrative team organically evolves out of the ministry participants.

Customize

BUILDING: Use the untraditional method of team building: You must start the ministry before you can start giving it away. Instead of initially recruiting leaders and team members, look for women with willing hearts who offer to *serve* in the ministry. Give these "servants" assignments and observe their performance. Develop the administrative team from dependable, reliable, teachable, and committed women who step up to help you launch the ministry.

This process takes time, but it's worth the effort. In the meantime, lower your expectations of what the ministry will accomplish. Only start with one or two projects and invite many women to participate—then wait for God to raise up leaders.

REMODELING: If you're replacing team members, follow the untraditional method described in "Building." Don't look *outside* the ministry for new leadership; look *within* it. The most qualified women to serve on the team are those who are already serving in and benefitting from the ministry.

REFURBISHING: You're looking for new ways to energize the team, so start by introducing a new untraditional team-building concept. Help the team develop their teams from within the ministry.

Tools

The Leadership Lessons of Jesus by Bob Briner and Ray Pritchard

Team-Building Project

List the names of family members or acquaintances to help you start the ministry while you're developing or rebuilding the administrative team.

1.

2.

3.

4.

What is the first step to starting the ministry or rebuilding the team?

Commit to taking that first step on this date: ___/___/___.

Leader to Leader

Team building takes time; ministry needs are now. Many ministries never get started because all the energy and time goes into trying to recruit and train a team. Often the momentum for the ministry dies because the focus is more on team building than ministry serving. Ministry needs don't always wait.

What is the ministry call God has put on your heart? Is it church members needing meals? A support group for teen pregnancy? An alternate path for girls considering abortion? A ministry to separated or divorced women? Infertility "mommies-in-waiting" ministry? Premarital counseling ministry? Mentoring ministry? Or maybe your church doesn't have a women's ministry. What is burdening your heart? _____

While you take the time developing a team, people in your church go hungry, pregnant teens make life-changing decisions—maybe choosing abortion, separated or divorced women remain devastated, infertile women feel alone, marriages take place without premarital counseling, the spiritually young lack mentors, or the women of your church miss the blessings of a churchwide women's ministry.

Luke 4:14–44 tells us that immediately following Jesus' baptism and time in the desert, He began teaching in the synagogues and healing the sick. He didn't wait for the ideal time or a group of people to help Him. There was ministry to do and He did it. God has put a call on your heart too—don't let that call become bogged down in developing a committee or team. Start the ministry and the helpers will come.

I know this goes against tradition that says you need a team before you can start a ministry, but read comments from Bob Briner and Ray Pritchard's book, *The Leadership Lessons of Jesus*, in their chapter on "Leading with and Through Traditions":

Tradition in and of itself is neither good nor bad. Wise leaders . . . must learn from the past but not be shackled by it. Tradition can sometimes become a chain if it restricts us from being open to new ideas and change, which is what Jesus meant when he said, "The Sabbath was made for man, not man for the Sabbath." A good manager *makes the existing system work for his or her advantage; a good* leader *questions the system, making the changes necessary for improvement. In Jesus, the ultimate leader, old things have passed away and all things have become new.*

Finishing Touches

If you're starting or rebuilding a ministry, ask yourself these questions:

- Are you willing to go it alone for a while?
- Do you believe God will meet your needs and provide until He brings the workers for the harvest?
- Will you let Jesus be your example and follow the ministry call, even without a team?
- Will you start small and let the ministry evolve as the right people reveal themselves as true leaders who can help you take the ministry to the next level?
- Do you have the courage?
- Do you trust your faith?
- Do you believe that God wants this ministry more than you want it?

I pray that your answer is "Yes, Lord, Yes!"

Mentoring Moment

When God is blessing a ministry, He meets all the needs in His timing.

~ CHAPTER 6 ~

Jesus Prayed for His Future Team

One of those days Jesus went out to a mountainside to pray, and spent the night praying to God. When morning came, he called his disciples to him and chose twelve of them whom he also designated apostles. — LUKE 6:12–13

The Cornerstone

Selecting His team was such an important and significant decision that Jesus secluded Himself and prayed all night on a mountaintop. When He came down from the mountain, Jesus *"chose"* His team—the twelve apostles. Perhaps during prayer, God revealed the 12 names from the numerous disciples following Jesus, so *"that they might be with him and that he might send them out to preach"* (Mark 3:14). Jesus knew this was the team He would prepare to carry on His earthly ministry after He was gone.

The Blueprint

An important point in Luke 6:12–13 is that Jesus *"designated"* the 12 as *"apostles."* Read this description of the term "apostle" from *The Revell Bible Dictionary:*

> *As a specialized title,* apostle *designates Jesus' twelve original disciples, who had a unique role in the founding of the church. They were envoys with authority, personally trained by Jesus himself. Jesus also commissioned them to "go and make disciples of all nations, baptizing them in the name*

*of the Father and of the Son and of the Holy Spirit, and teaching them
to obey everything I have commanded you"* (Mt. 28:18-20).

Choosing people to assume the important role of designated *apostle* on Jesus'
team couldn't be a decision made on a whim. Only God could provide the
wisdom Jesus needed to select the right men. Only God can provide the
wisdom you need to select the right women for the important role of designated
shepherd coach.

Customize

BUILDING: Pray expectantly and with faith that God will provide an
administrative team of shepherd coaches. Pray His will is done in the ministry
as it is in heaven and that God will meet your needs. Then wait on the Lord.

REMODELING: Pray for wisdom as you replace or add to the team. In your
remodel, designate team members as shepherd coaches.

REFURBISHING: Discuss the idea of the team being designated as shepherd
coaches. Pray with the shepherd coaches as they pray for God to develop their
teams.

Tools

Let me share an expectant prayer for you to pray:

> *Lord, You gifted me with this ministry, and I know You don't want me to
> lead it alone. Your Word tells us that two are better than one and the church
> functions as the physical body with many parts working as one. Please give
> me wisdom and discernment as to who You have picked to be my immediate
> team members. Who do You want me to pour into? Give me eyes to see
> beyond the exterior and look into people's hearts. Instill into me courage and
> boldness to approach those who might be potential team members and show
> loving kindness to those You reveal to me aren't the right women for the job.
> I am Your willing servant, and my desire is to serve You and select a team
> for You to build. Thank You for caring about these things and that I can
> come to You with my smallest concern. In Jesus' name, I pray, amen.*

Team-Building Project

Observe women currently serving in your church and ministry who are: dependable, compatible, passionate, humble, and committed. Wait, watch, pray, and jot down names here. Pray over this list daily. Focus your prayers for discernment and wisdom on those names that repeatedly bring peace to your spirit. Continue adding to and praying over the list.

Possible Shepherd Coaches

1.   5.

2.   6.

3.   7.

4.   8.

Leader to Leader

God knew the mentoring ministry needs before I did, so I prayed for Him to bring just the right women to serve. I spent many hours praying for wisdom and discernment, and for God to put in my path women with the potential to help in the ministry. Then there she would be—maybe I would see her sitting in church, or chatting out on the church patio, or browsing at the local Christian bookstore, or shopping at the grocery store. God was faithful to answer my prayers for a team, and He will answer yours too.

Pray for who God wants on your prospective team. Pray for patience with this process because it will take time. My error in the beginning was to rush ahead of God instead of waiting on Him. When you select the team members, continue praying for them. Discover their needs, both personally and in the ministry, and let them know you're lifting them up in prayer. We'll talk later about team members praying for each other. For now, pray for God to reveal your future team.

Finishing Touches

It's impossible to be an effective leader without:

- A faithful daily quiet time.
- Membership and regular attendance at church.
- Participation in a group that encourages spiritual growth and accountability.

Be sure you've incorporated the above three spiritual disciplines into your life before considering adding a new role—like leading a ministry and team.

Mentoring Moment

God has gifted you with an important role requiring significant time spent with Him. Schedule God into your activities, or your activities will schedule God out.

Jesus Called His Team

He saw James son of Zebedee and his brother John in a boat, preparing their nets. Without delay he called them, and they left their father Zebedee in the boat with the hired men and followed him.   — MARK 1:19–20

The Cornerstone

Jesus chose and personally invited the disciples to join Him (Mark 1:16–20; 2:14; 3:13–19). Without hesitation, He handpicked and *"called"* His team by boldly approaching each one and offering the opportunity to serve with Him. Jesus sought out and asked men to follow Him and be His trusted teammates. No one He called turned Him down!

The Blueprint

Jesus didn't ask who wanted to be on His team, use a recruiter, post a sign-up sheet, or send a messenger or letter. He didn't coerce, beg, persuade, manipulate, or force. Jesus was proactive and intentional in selecting His team. He knew exactly who He wanted and went after them. Many people were followers, but He only asked a select few to be in His immediate circle of training and mentoring.

Customize

BUILDING: In the last chapter, you made a list of potential shepherd coaches, and you've been praying over the list. It's time to "call" the team on the phone or approach in person the ones you've chosen and arrange for an interview. During your initial conversation with the prospective shepherd coach:

- Tell her you've observed her heart for service and would like to meet to discuss a service opportunity.
- Give a summary of the position you have in mind. You don't need to provide detailed information during the initial contact. You're not asking for a decision on the phone.
- If she would like to meet, establish a time and place.
- Honor her request if she says no or wants to pray and call you back.
- If she doesn't call you back, unless there was an emergency, she probably didn't know how to tell you, no.
- If she calls back and wants more information, give her a summary of the opportunity and again offer to meet with her. Assure her it's an information-gathering meeting for you both and you won't need a commitment at that time.
- Never talk someone into a meeting or taking a position, regardless of how perfect she seems for the role or how badly you need the position filled. There's a difference between modest and hesitant. Pray you have discernment to tell the difference.

REMODELING: You may have problems with current team members because of initially minimizing the commitment or the extent of the responsibilities, or persuading someone to serve whose heart wasn't in being on the team. Think back to how you developed the team compared to the suggestions in this chapter and in "Building." Make appropriate changes in how you "call" future team members.

REFURBISHING: If the team is running smoothly, you probably had good parameters and guidelines for selecting team members. Discuss with the team how to "call" their future teams.

Tools

Jesus had divine wisdom. We have divine access, but not omnipotent wisdom. Take steps to assure that serving together is a good fit. Approach meeting with a prospective team member as an interview with a plan and focus; otherwise, you might have a nice chat over coffee but still not know about each other or discuss the service opportunity.

Don't feel you need to put every woman who wants to serve with you on the team. Do your homework. Use the following tools to help discuss pertinent information during the interview.

- When you meet to discuss the service opportunity, use the *interview questionnaire* below to help you stay on track and on task. Feel free to adapt it to your interviewing style.
- The question about tithing in question 2 might be difficult for you to ask, but it's an important indicator of spiritual maturity and willingness to serve God wholeheartedly. If she's not cheerfully giving her money to God, she won't cheerfully give her time.
- The Service Opportunity Description discussed in question 5 provides details about the position under discussion. See chapter 14, pages 98–99, for guidelines in how to write a Service Opportunity Description and examples.
- "The Top Ten Do's and Don'ts When Interviewing" are tips for conducting the interview.

INTERVIEW QUESTIONNAIRE

Name _____ Position Presented _____

Date _____

After initial greeting, open your time together in prayer.

1. Ask her to tell "Her Story"
     Accepting Christ
     Coming to your church
     Family
     If she has a husband, is he a believer?

2. Spiritual Maturity
     Is she a member and regular attendee of your church?
     Is she in a small group or Bible study?
     Does she have a daily quiet time?
     Does she tithe?
     Has she taken any classes your church offers?

3. Is she serving in another ministry and how will that impact her serving on the team?

4. What is her SHAPE (spiritual gifts, heart, abilities, personality, experiences)?

5. Provide a Service Opportunity Description for the position that best fits her SHAPE.
     Is this a position that interests her?
     Will she commit to the requirements, responsibilities, and duration?
     Why does she want to serve in this position?

6. Does she have any questions?

7. Both of you pray about the opportunity for several days and set a date for her to call you back.
Close in prayer.

THE TOP TEN DO'S AND DON'TS WHEN INTERVIEWING

DON'T

1. Interview on the phone or by email
2. Do all the talking
3. Gloss over responsibilities
4. Minimize the commitment
5. Think family life won't matter
6. Just give information
7. Minimize red flags
8. Skip anything on the interview form
9. Make a decision during the interview
10. Decide the next day or call her

DO

1. Meet in person
2. Ask questions and let her talk
3. Review the Service Opportunity Description
4. Clearly state your expectations
5. Find out if her husband is agreeable to her serving and where he is spiritually
6. Let her ask questions
7. Address problem issues
8. Conversationally discuss all points
9. Both take a minimum of three days to pray
10. Ask her to call you back at an agreed upon time

Team-Building Project

1. If you've never interviewed before, interview a friend or family member using the Interview Questionnaire (under previous "Tools") before interviewing your first potential team member. During your friend or family member practice interview, try tactfully and kindly telling someone a position doesn't seem right for her, and develop a gracious response if she chooses not to serve on your team.

2. When you have a team, share these tools with them to use in interviewing their own team members. Have them practice interviewing each other.

3. Read chapter 14 for tips on how to write and use the Service Opportunity Description. Then write a Service Opportunity Description when you're ready to interview for a position.

Leader to Leader

I learned the lesson of "calling" a team the hard way. As I mentioned in chapter 2, the first team chose me instead of me choosing them. If a woman wanted to be on the administrative team, I brought her on the team to do what she told me she did best. Big mistake! The Lord whittled my initial team of 12 down to three, and I learned how to follow Jesus' example of selecting a team.

While remodeling our team of three and rebuilding a future team, I vowed not to repeat the same mistakes twice. If you're in a smaller church, three or four may be the perfect number for your team. Between the four of us on my "revised team," we accomplished the essential ministry work, and I watched and waited for the Lord to reveal additional team members. Until then, we did without. Jesus had an "inner core" of three disciples, Peter, James, and John, so I was off to a good start, and so are you if you're starting out with one or two team members. As women joined the ministry, I approached those I wanted to interview for the vacant shepherd coach roles, and I developed and used the Interview Questionnaire.

I remember sitting at church in front of three women from the mentoring ministry when God put on my heart that they were women of prayer who would be valuable in the ministry. After church, I turned around and affirmed their love for prayer and asked if they would like to talk to me about serving in that capacity. Their response was, "Really! You think I could do that?" One of them went on to become the *prayer warrior shepherd coach* and the other two served on her team. The Lord tells us that we have not because we ask not (James 4:2), so keep your eyes open around church for possible team members.

Finishing Touches

- Jesus personally asked each disciple to join His team.
- Telling someone you see her potential and are considering her for the team is affirming!
- When offering a team position, meet face to face rather than using email, Facebook, or texting.
- Don't feel rejected if she says no; it just means this isn't the right role for her. Graciously move on to ask someone else.
- Don't call her back after the interview, even though you'll be anxious and curious to know her answer. Wait for her to call you on the specified day; her timeliness or failure to call will say a lot about how responsible and reliable she'll be as a leader.

Mentoring Moment

It's easier doing without than working with someone who isn't ready for leadership.

Jesus Chose a Specific Number

He appointed twelve—designating them apostles.   —MARK 3:14

The Cornerstone

Jesus chose 12 team members. We don't know why He chose 12, except perhaps that is what the Father told Him to do. Even after Judas' betrayal and suicide and Jesus' death and resurrection, the remaining apostles recruited a 12th, *"May another take his* [Judas'] *place of leadership"* (Acts 1:20). Twelve was the perfect number for Jesus' team (Acts 1:15–26).

The Blueprint

We tend to think the more people on the team the better: more productivity, more ideas, more hands to do the work. However, more on an administrative team can also have negative results: more chaos, more confusion, more distractions. Instead, select a number for the administrative team that you can efficiently and effectively nurture and lead, a number that fits the ministry needs and size of your church.

Customize

BUILDING: To arrive at the number of shepherd coaches for the administrative team:

1. Determine the major areas the ministry will be serving—limit to six to eight for a mid- to large-size church; three to four may be sufficient for a smaller church.
2. Group similar areas together.
3. Choose a shepherd coach for each area.

REMODELING: If you have more than eight areas for shepherd coaches, consolidate by combining several related areas under one shepherd coach. If you have more areas than you have potential shepherd coach candidates, also merge similar areas until you recruit more team members.

REFURBISHING: If you're comfortable with the number on the current team, don't make changes. As shepherd coaches leave or step down, use that as an opportunity to reevaluate.

Tools

To start the process of determining the ideal number of shepherd coaches for the administrative team, list the areas you oversee as a women's ministry visionary director.

1.	7.
2.	8.
3.	9.
4.	10.
5.	11.
6.	12.

Now list any areas you would like to add to the ministry in the future.

1.

2.

3.

4.

5.

Team-Building Project

1. Using the lists you compiled under "Tools," group like areas together. For example:
- Bible study for singles, working women, moms, seniors, small groups, churchwide women's study, etc., would all come under "Bible Study."
- Missions and evangelism fall under "Outreach."
- Teas, retreats, conferences, banquets, ladies' night out, etc., would all come under "Special Events."

2. Continue this process until you have six to eight groups (or three to four for smaller churches).

3. Title each group, and these become the shepherd coach positions on the administrative team. List them here:

1.   5.

2.   6.

3.   7.

4.   8.

4. If you're building a team, these are the shepherd coach positions you recruit to fill. If you're remodeling or refurbishing and you currently have too many areas under one coach, use this process to create a new position. If you have too many shepherd coaches on the team, merge similar areas under one shepherd coach. You may have to wait for natural attrition to consolidate, but it becomes your goal. As an example, the administrative team of Anywhere Church Women's Ministry is comprised of the following shepherd coaches:
- Bible Study
- Woman to Woman Mentoring
- Support Groups
- Special Events
- Finance
- Outreach

Leader to Leader

When I first developed a team, I thought more was better. If Jesus had 12 on His team, then I should too if I was going to follow His model. I learned that Jesus could handle 12 because, of course, He was Jesus; but for me 12 was a committee, not a team. The model I needed to follow was not the exact number that Jesus had, but how He arrived at that number. For the work He had to do in the time He had to spend, 12 was the perfect number for Him. Determine an efficient, productive size for your administrative team based on the work you have to do and the size of your church.

Finishing Touches

- Consider the example of building a house: the contractor selects a foreman, who selects a team of specialists to report to him on their particular area of the building project: pouring cement, framing, roofing, wiring for electricity, plumbing, and painting. These specialists each select and oversee a team of workers. How effective would the foreman be if *all* the workers on the project reported directly to him and he had to oversee each one? The house might never be built.
- God is the Contractor who selects you, the ministry visionary director foreman, to build a team and ministry. You determine the number of specialist shepherd coaches for the administrative team by the scope and diversity of the work you oversee. Then each shepherd coach selects and oversees a team using the same procedure. A team and ministry are built!

Mentoring Moment

The bigger the team, the more difficult to manage.

Jesus Recruited Unlikely People

As he walked along, he saw Levi son of Alphaeus sitting at the tax collector's booth. "Follow me," Jesus told him, and Levi got up and followed him.

—MARK 2:14

The Cornerstone

Jesus saw potential in common fishermen, telling them soon they would be fishers of men (Mark 1:17). Then He added Matthew, a shrewd and hated tax collector, along with Matthew's political opposite, Simon the Zealot. They didn't appear to be likely candidates for Jesus' team, but Jesus saw their potential regardless of current situations, circumstances, or careers. Luke 5:1–11 is an example of Jesus observing Simon Peter, James, and John following instructions and respecting Jesus and His authority, even when they didn't fully understand His plan (5:5).

The Blueprint

The ragtag group of men Jesus chose for His leadership team should encourage us that with Christ as our Ultimate Leader, we *all* have potential to lead. Often, it's the same group of people doing all the work all the time. Keep a vigilant eye for those who show leadership potential even though they may not fit the "leader" mold. Jesus chose unlikely people and developed them to reach their potential for specific roles. He didn't limit himself to seeking human opinion or approval, and He didn't judge by externals. He looked at each team member individually and saw their future potential, not their current status.

Customize

Building: Consider a wide variety of people for the team. Return to the list you made in the "Team-Building Project" (chap. 6, p. 55) where you observed women serving in your church and ministry and jotted down names of those who stood out above the rest for being committed, dependable, compatible, passionate, and humble. Do you see any unlikely people on that list? If not, why not? If everyone on your list is similar or just like you, you won't have a balanced team.

REMODELING: The team may be unbalanced and lacking in diversity. As you replace or add new team members, look at inner, not outer, qualities.

REFURBISHING: Observe the team to see if you have a diversified group. If you haven't taken the risk to include an "unlikely" team member, make a commitment to do so with your next team opening.

Tools

In *The Maxwell Leadership Bible*, John C. Maxwell suggests you can learn valuable lessons from Jesus by asking yourself the following six questions when selecting a team member:
   1. What positive qualities exist that may be seen as negative behavior?
   2. Do the individuals show initiative, even if it has been misdirected?
   3. Would these people add positive chemistry and unique value if placed on the team?
   4. Are they hungry to become something more than what they are now?
   5. Do they demonstrate passion that could be redirected?
   6. Could they play a needed role on the team?

Team-Building Project

Revisit the list you made in chapter 6 of possible shepherd coaches (p. 55). Based on the previous six questions in "Tools," who isn't on the list that you should consider? Who did you put on the list for all the wrong reasons? Rewrite your revised list here:

1.   5.

2.   6.

3.   7.

4.   8.

Pray and ask God to open your *eyes to the people* He puts into your path and to give you the courage to consider people different from *yourself*—even the unlikely, improbable ones. Your list may become shorter or longer, but continue to keep your options and heart open. There is no greater surprise than to watch someone blossom who you never thought could do the job.

Leader to Leader

Occasionally when I told a ministry colleague that I was considering someone for a shepherd coach position, the response was: "Oh, I can't see her doing that." Or, "She's really busy." Or, "She works full time." Or, "She doesn't seem like a leader." You get the picture.

We tend to have our own prerequisites regarding who can lead, but often those thoughts derive from our own perception of what we could or couldn't do if we were in that situation. I prayed to keep an open mind and offered the position, without prejudging, to people God put on my heart or in my path. As a result, our administrative team was comprised of all ages and various walks of life, and that kept us balanced.

Probably the most "unlikely" person on the team was me! I had no experience directing a ministry, had never attended any women's functions or served on a ministry team, and initially, wasn't even sure I wanted to work with women. All I had on my ministry résumé was a "Feed my sheep" call from the Lord, a vision of a mentoring ministry, leadership skills, willingness to do whatever it took, and being a seminary student. If I had come into your office telling you my "Feed my sheep" story and said I felt led to start a women's mentoring ministry, what would have been your immediate response?

Thankfully, the pastors to whom I told my story gave me an opportunity. They caught my vision and encouraged me to take the steps to start a new ministry at Saddleback. You're reading this book today—and thousands of women around the world have experienced Woman to Woman Mentoring— because those pastors took a chance with an "unlikely" person. Keep your mind, heart, and options open. Today I'm known as the woman who has a heart for women. God can change a willing servant's heart.

Finishing Touches

〰️ Every Christian is a leader whose life should lead others to Christ. As daily news of corrupt leadership bombards us, many women look at leadership as a bad thing. They don't see themselves as leaders and the word *leader* intimidates and scares them. Yet, many of these same women run complicated businesses, have demanding jobs, or manage households while balancing numerous aspects of a family's daily life. They are leaders. It just takes someone to believe in them and show them how to apply their daily leadership skills to ministry.

〰️ The world's leadership criteria aren't God's criteria (1 Samuel 16:7). Jesus looked for heart issues in those who served with Him. A good candidate is—

- 〰️ Willing
- 〰️ Teachable
- 〰️ Trainable
- 〰️ Dependable
- 〰️ Capable
- 〰️ Committed

Mentoring Moment

Don't be fooled by outside appearances (Galatians 2:6) or someone who "seems" right for the position. Think outside the box and inside the heart.

~ CHAPTER 10 ~

Jesus Chose People with Different Gifts and Talents

These are the twelve he appointed: Simon (to whom he gave the name Peter);
James son of Zebedee and his brother John (to them he gave the name
Boanerges, which means Sons of Thunder); Andrew, Philip, Bartholomew,
Matthew, Thomas, James son of Alphaeus, Thaddaeus, Simon the Zealot
and Judas Iscariot, who betrayed him. —MARK 3:16–19

The Cornerstone

- ⌁ Jesus was a carpenter, a religious teacher, a prophet, and a rabbi—His team members were fishermen, a tax collector, and a political zealot.
- ⌁ Jesus was a scriptural scholar—the disciples He designated apostles were spiritual neophytes.
- ⌁ Jesus was the meeting of grace and truth—His disciples were quick tempered and doubters.

Jesus chose these men to be His future replacement. They were a slice of life: a representation of the community. People could relate to them. So Jesus, the Lord of lords and King of kings, chose a team of extremely ordinary men to serve in a phenomenally extraordinary ministry.

The Blueprint

There's a saying that if two people are exactly alike, one of them isn't needed!

Humanly, we migrate towards people who think and act like us, but teams comprised of mirror images of the leader are ineffective, cliquey, and constrained. A diverse team is versatile, creative, innovative, and challenges the leader to work with people who differ from her. A healthy, well-balanced team will have members representing:

- A wide age range
- All seasons of life
- Varied personalities
- Different spiritual gifts

Customize

BUILDING: Have each prospective team member take a personality and spiritual gifts assessment. Assure her that these are not pass-or-fail tests, but tools to help you and other team members get to know her better. You take the tests, too, and share everyone's results with each other. The team isn't complete until you have a representation from different generations, life stages, personalities, and spiritual gifts.

REMODELING: At a team meeting or retreat, give current team members a personality and spiritual gifts assessment and discuss everyone's results. As you add or replace team members, give them the tests also. The team learns the results, and the new member learns the assessment results of existing team members. This helps bridge the "getting to know each other" phase.

REFURBISHING: Have fun taking and discussing the personality and spiritual gift assessments with the team. This helps everyone understand and work with each other more effectively and efficiently.

Tools

If possible, give the books to each team member to read and discuss as a team.
Wired That Way by Florence and Marita Littauer
Wired That Way Assessment, available through CLASServices, Inc.,
    1-800-433-6633 or www.classervices.com.

The Four Elements of Success by Laurie Beth Jones
Finding Your Spiritual Gifts: Wagner-Modified Houts Questionnaire by C. Peter Wagner *Finding Your Place in Ministry: An Online Spiritual Gifts Inventory* available at www.buildingchurch.net/g2s.htm.

Team-Building Project

In her book, *The Four Elements of Success*, Laurie Beth Jones offers a simple personality profile based on the characteristics of the elements earth, wind, fire, and water. Jones suggests that every personality has leadership qualities, and she explores how personality differences affect team dynamics. Jones uses a number of fun and revealing exercises to help teams get clear about their individual identities. One of her most popular exercises has each "element" reveal their strengths, their challenges in working with the other "elements," and then discuss why they need each other. To obtain information about these exercises to use with your team, visit her Web sites:
Path Elements Profile:
    http://www.lauriebethjones.com/find/four_elements.html
The Elemental Team Challenge:
    http://www.lauriebethjones.com/advance/elemental/challenge.html
The Path Mission Download:
    http://www.lauriebethjones.com/find/creating_mission.html

Leader to Leader

Tools such as personality and spiritual gifts assessments can help your team of vastly different people learn to work cohesively with each other. For example, I am a visionary who dreams big and thinks anything is possible. A cautious type personality might point out possible roadblocks in my visions. Before understanding personalities, I dismissed this cautious person as negative and uncooperative. But after we took the personality assessments, I learned she was proactively trying to ensure the success of the project. The excitement and enthusiasm of an action-oriented visionary can appear unrealistic, irresponsible, and impetuous to a person who processes and analyzes all options and details before taking action. A leader needs to surround herself with people who excel in areas that aren't her strengths.

When the team members understand and appreciate personality differences, they're less reactive and critical of each other and more cooperative and tolerant.

Finishing Touches

- Read 1 Corinthians 12:12–30 and Ephesians 4:11–13, which emphasize the importance of unifying our various God-given gifts.
- Take a personality test and discover how others might perceive you as a leader. Work on strengthening your positive traits and tempering those that might be offensive.
- Know your spiritual gifts and surround yourself with those who have the gifts you don't. For example, leaders are often notoriously short on compassion and mercy—essential components to the relational aspect of a team. You need to have people on your team who are strong in those areas.
- The more varied the team, the more versatile and creative it will be. This also challenges you to work with women different from you.
- Each personality has perceived good and bad sides depending on who is looking. Understanding that a person's comments or actions that grate on you might just be a personality difference will help you work with her more peacefully and effectively.
- To recruit people at various ages and seasons of life, visit the areas of your church where these women meet. If you have a seniors ministry, let them know about the team opportunities, and do the same with other ministries (i.e. young adults, singles, family, missions).

Mentoring Moment

The aged are wise and experienced and the young are eager and energetic. Healthy, well-balanced teams are diverse.

Jesus Recruited with a Purpose

As Jesus walked beside the Sea of Galilee, he saw Simon and his brother Andrew casting a net into the lake, for they were fishermen, "Come, follow me," Jesus said, "and I will make you fishers of men." At once they left their nets and followed him. —MARK 1:16–18

He said to them "Let us go into the next towns, that I may preach there also, because for this purpose I have come forth." —MARK 1:38 (NKJV)

The Cornerstone

Jesus recruited team members for unique roles that fit their specific gifts and talents. Each one had something to contribute toward accomplishing the purpose of Jesus' ministry. Jesus took this group of seemingly misfit individuals and molded them into a synergistic, unified team that loved one another and worked effectively together spreading the gospel.

The Blueprint

Recruiting with purpose requires knowing the purpose of the ministry and of each ministry position. Developing a mission statement for the ministry and a one-sentence purpose statement for each team position helps clarify the goal and direction of the ministry and the role and expectations of each shepherd coach. If you can't determine a purpose statement for a position, evaluate whether you need the position.

Customize

BUILDING: Determine the ministry objectives and the purpose of each of the six to eight (or three to four) shepherd coach positions you arrived at in the "Team-Building Project" in chapter 8 (p. 67).

REMODELING: If you haven't written a ministry mission statement and a purpose statement for the shepherd coach positions, write them now to guide you in rebuilding the ministry and the team.

REFURBISHING: It's time to update the ministry mission statement and determine the purpose for each shepherd coach position. Over time, the ministry changes and evolves from when you first started leading. Let the shepherd coaches help with the revisions.

Tools

MINISTRY MISSION STATEMENT

In the *Woman to Woman Mentoring Ministry Coordinator's Guide*, I provide guidelines and suggestions for writing a ministry mission statement.

- Answer the question, Why and for what purpose does this ministry exist?
- State that purpose in two or three sentences.
- Use general language, avoiding colloquialisms and "inside" terms.

EXAMPLE—
WOMAN TO WOMAN MENTORING MINISTRY MISSION STATEMENT

To give the women of Saddleback Church the opportunity to experience joy and growth in their Christian lives by participating in one-on-one supporting and encouraging mentoring friendships.

ADMINISTRATIVE TEAM PURPOSE STATEMENT

The administrative team purpose statement should answer the question, Why do I need a team of shepherd coaches and how will they enhance the ministry?

EXAMPLE—
PURPOSE: To assist the ministry visionary director in leading the ministry and developing teams to serve the women of our church.

SHEPHERD COACH PURPOSE STATEMENT
The purpose statement for each shepherd coach position you're considering should answer the question, Why is this position needed on the administrative team? Notice the purpose of the special events shepherd coach is to develop a team and not do special events on her own.

EXAMPLE—
PURPOSE: To shepherd and coach a team that provides opportunities for fun, fellowship, spiritual growth, and learning for the women of Anywhere Church and the community.

Team-Building Project

1. Using the guidelines and examples under "Tools," write:

Ministry Mission Statement

_____

_____

_____

_____

Administrative Team Purpose Statement

_____

_____

_____

_____

2. Beside the numbers below, write purpose statements for each potential shepherd coach. You may find that two different shepherd coaches have similar or overlapping purposes, allowing you to consolidate them under one shepherd coach. Or a shepherd coach has multiple and unrelated purposes

and you need to create another shepherd coach position. Remember, you aren't writing the Service Opportunity Description, just the reason the position exists. You should be able to state the purpose in one sentence.

1.

2.

3.

4.

5.

6.

7.

8.

Leader to Leader

When you interview a prospective shepherd coach, share with her the ministry mission statement, the administrative team purpose statement, and the purpose statement for her specific role and how it fits into the ministry visions, goals, and operations. Ask her purpose in wanting to join the administrative team. Why does she want to serve in this capacity? Then listen carefully because it's essential that her purpose and the ministry purpose are compatible.

For example, if someone tells you she wants to be a shepherd coach so she can work on her leadership skills, or she wants to work closer with you and learn from you—both are red-flag warning signs. She just told you her purpose in serving is to benefit *her* and not what she can contribute to the ministry.

Finishing Touches

When team members' gifts and personalities match the purpose of their positions, you'll have a team much like the varied team that Jesus compiled. In our Anywhere Church Women's Ministry example:

- The Bible study shepherd coach may be more spiritually mature than the financial shepherd coach, whose strong organizational skills occasionally clash with the visionary director's plans.
- The support groups shepherd coach is deeply sensitive, compassionate, and perhaps quiet.
- The special events shepherd coach is outgoing and gregarious.
- The outreach shepherd coach insists *every* event is evangelistic, which could be uncomfortable for other shepherd coaches.
- The Woman to Woman Mentoring shepherd coach wants everyone to be a mentor.
- Shepherd coaches will be single or married, working or at home, small business owners or CEOs, schoolteachers or crossing guards, old or young.
- Regardless of their differences, it's the common goal, objective, and purpose of the ministry that unites them as one team working together to accomplish the mission of the ministry.

Mentoring Moment

"Teams, by their nature, require specialists. Specialists often differ in personality and view. Team members combine their strengths to help one another to grow and to change their world. Such a diversified team may be tougher to lead —but then training lions is more exciting than feeding goldfish!"

—*The Leadership Bible* (ZONDERVAN)

CHAPTER 12

Jesus Was Organized

Jesus directed them to have all the people sit down in groups on the green grass. So they sat down in groups of hundreds and fifties. — MARK 6:39–40

The Cornerstone

In feeding the five thousand, Jesus displayed organizational skills to His team by giving them specific instructions for seating the people. Instead of randomly feeding an out-of-control crowd, He had the people divided into groups of specific numbers and delegated specific tasks to the disciples. Jesus didn't step in and feed the crowd Himself, but instructed His team, *"You give them something to eat"* (Mark 6:37). Scripture records Jesus doing three things: thanking God for the bread, breaking the bread, and dividing the fish. Then the apostles delivered the food and cleaned up.

The Blueprint

Leaders create a calming sense of order with a system and procedure that are simple, functional, and allow everyone to understand her responsibility and use her gifts. An organization team chart meets these specifications by showing how team members' roles fit into the ministry's operation and how everyone shares the workload. Women serving in the ministry also need to know who to go to for questions and guidance because the ministry visionary director can't be the only "go-to" person.

In ministry, the team chart isn't a discriminating or hierarchy tool—it depicts a method of organization and delegation that God introduced as early as Moses to help instill leadership order, structure, and responsibility in ministry. Moses' father-in-law, Jethro, the Bible's first recorded organizational consultant, helped Moses see the value of organized delegation.

> *"Select capable men from all the people—men who fear God, trustworthy men who hate dishonest gain—and appoint them as officials over thousands, hundreds, fifties and tens. Have them serve as judges for the people at all times, but have them bring every difficult case to you; the simple cases they can decide themselves. That will make your load lighter, because they will share it with you. If you do this and God so commands, you will be able to stand the strain, and all these people will go home satisfied."*
>
> *Moses listened to his father-in-law and did everything he said. He chose capable men from all Israel and made them leaders of the people, officials over thousands, hundreds, fifties and tens.* —Exodus 18:21–25

Deuteronomy 1:9–18 also explains how Moses applied Jethro's wise advice so that Moses, the "ministry visionary director," wouldn't burn out and the people would be better served by a team of leaders.

Acts 6:1–7 confirms that Jesus' team, the 12 disciples, understood the value and greater good of organization and delegation and later applied these concepts in their own teams.

> *In those days when the number of disciples was increasing, the Grecian Jews among them complained against the Hebraic Jews because their widows were being overlooked in the daily distribution of food. So the Twelve gathered all the disciples together and said, "It would not be right for us to neglect the ministry of the word of God in order to wait on tables. Brothers choose seven men from among you who are known to be full of the Spirit and wisdom. We will turn this responsibility over to them and will give our attention to prayer and the ministry of the word."*
>
> *This proposal pleased the whole group. They chose Stephen, a man full of faith and of the Holy Spirit; also Philip, Procorus, Nicanor, Timon, Parmenas, and Nicolas from Antioch, a convert to Judaism. They presented*

these men to the apostles, who prayed and laid their hands on them.
So the word of God spread. The number of disciples in Jerusalem increased
rapidly, and a large number of priests became obedient to the faith.

Reread the above scenarios described in the Scripture passages and personalize them to your situation and size.

Another helpful organizational tool is a ministry binder for each shepherd coach. The ministry binder transfers to successors for a complete history and record of what has transpired previously in the shepherd coach's team.

Customize

BUILDING: In the appendix you'll find a Jethro-style team chart to complete with the six to eight (four to six) shepherd coach positions that will comprise the administrative team and create a ministry binder for each of these positions. (See the "Tools" and "Team-Building Project" sections below.)

REMODELING: Introduce the concept of team charts and binders. (See the "Tools" and "Team-Building Project" sections below, and the appendix.) Soon you'll have shepherd coaches forming their own teams using the same organizational parameters.

REFURBISHING: If you haven't used team charts or team binders, instill these tools now. This will prepare the shepherd coaches for organizing their teams and utilizing team charts for their area of service. (See the "Tools" and "Team-Building Project" sections below, and the appendix.) You may incur some resistance, but don't let that deter you. Remind them that the goal is to have a team like Jesus, and He was organized. Let the shepherd coaches help design the binders and their contents.

Tools

In the appendix, you will find sample team charts for Anywhere Church and blank charts for you and the team to individualize and customize.

The shepherd coaches are the first level of leadership under the ministry visionary director and they comprise the administrative team that the ministry visionary director:

- meets with
- counsels
- trains
- loves
- teaches
- mentors
- retreats with

The shepherd coaches learn from the ministry visionary director and develop a team of apprentices and team leaders. Each shepherd coach determines the areas where she needs team leaders and recruits women to fill those positions that the shepherd coach:

- meets with
- counsels
- trains
- loves
- teaches
- mentors
- retreats with

Each team leader has responsibilities in her area and recruits a team of coordinators. The coordinators then develop and recruit teams of helpers from the ministry members seeking an opportunity to serve.

Ministry visionary director — shepherd coach — team leader — coordinator — are all leadership roles. In summary:

- The *ministry visionary director*'s team is the *shepherd coaches*.
- The *shepherd coaches*' teams are the *team leaders*.
- The *team leaders*' teams are the *coordinators*.
- The *coordinators* develop and work with teams of *helpers*.

The size of these teams will vary with the size of your church. You may start out with only shepherd coaches and helpers. As the ministry grows, add the next levels of leadership.

Team-Building Project

1. Read Exodus 18:21–25, Deuteronomy 1:9–18, and Mark 9:33–37.
2. Start customizing and using the team charts in the appendix.
3. Teach the shepherd coaches how to use this organizational tool so they can create and implement the team charts with their team leaders, who will then do the same with their coordinators.
4. If your budget allows, purchase a ministry binder with dividers for each shepherd coach. Ask an artistic or creative person in the ministry to design a cover for the binders. Label the divider tabs with topics such as: team meeting minutes, calendar of events, notes, team charts, service opportunity descriptions, and correspondence. Then ask each shepherd coach to label several tabs specific to her area of service. Remind the team that the binder stays with the ministry to be passed along to successors.

Leader to Leader

I first presented the team chart delegation concept and ministry binders to the team at "The Team That Jesus Built" retreat. Some of them rolled their eyes protesting that this was way over their heads. Women serving on teams come from all walks of life and many aren't familiar with organization and delegation charts, so you'll need to explain how the team will benefit from using them.

If you're still wondering yourself how the team charts will help, maybe you'll identify with the following scenario. When I arrive at the airport to speak at an event, it's often the frazzled and exhausted women's ministry director who picks me up while continuously on a cell phone putting out all the event-planning fires back at the church. Then when we get to the church, I see only a handful of helpers. When I ask, "Where are all the helpers?" the reply is often, "Oh, they'll be here tomorrow. They had things they needed to do tonight." My heart breaks for this ministry director because I know she probably hasn't learned to delegate responsibility and the women of her church haven't learned how to serve selflessly. She's trying to do everything herself.

Team charts are a visual of the workload evenly distributed among leaders and teams responsible for specific areas of service. Instead of doing all the work herself, the ministry visionary director can attend and enjoy events and maybe gives thanks for the food and break the bread.

Finishing Touches

- Multiplying leadership allows the ministry visionary director to be a servant leader who touches more lives than she could on her own. If she's ever unavailable to serve, the ministry work can still continue.
- The ministry visionary director mentors the shepherd coaches who teach what they've been taught to their team leaders who teach what they've been taught to their coordinators. That's my definition of mentoring: Teaching what you've been taught so you can train those God puts in your path, so they can teach what you taught them to those God puts in their path. . . .
- The term *shepherd coach* derives from shepherd as a nurturer and coach as a teacher and trainer. As the ministry visionary director, your role is to empower shepherd coaches to assume these roles with their team leaders, who look to their shepherd coach for guidance, direction, and empowerment as they lead their coordinators.
- Don't expect everyone immediately to embrace organization or "get it." The team charts probably will be the topic of many future meetings and discussion, but it's a place to start.

Mentoring Moment

Effective leaders are organized. The goal of organization isn't to make the ministry run like a business, but to utilize effective business tools and adapt them to ministry.

Jesus Didn't Minimize the Sacrifice

Any of you who does not give up everything he has cannot be my disciple.

—LUKE 14:33

He called the crowd to him along with his disciples and said: "If anyone would come after me, he must deny himself and take up his cross and follow me."

—MARK 8:34

They pulled their boats up on shore, left everything and followed him.

—LUKE 5:11

The Cornerstone

Jesus set high standards for participating on His team, and He spoke often about the cost (Matthew 8:18–22; Luke 9:57–62; 14:25–33). In Luke 18:18–25, a rich young ruler asked Jesus what it would take to inherit eternal life and be His follower. Jesus' words cut straight to the heart, "*Sell everything you have and give to the poor, and you will have treasure in heaven. Then come, follow me*" (v. 22). The rich man's response: "*When he heard this, he became very sad, because he was a man of great wealth. Jesus looked at him and said, 'How hard it is for the rich to enter the kingdom of God!'*" (vv. 23–24).

When Peter pointed out: "*We have left all we had to follow you!*" (v. 28), Jesus replied, "*I tell you the truth . . . no one who has left home or wife or brothers or parents or children for the sake of the kingdom of God will fail to receive many times as much in this age and, in the age to come, eternal life*" (vv. 29–30).

The Blueprint

The *Leadership Bible* (Zondervan) comments on Luke 14:25–35 and the sacrifice required to be a disciple of Christ:

> *Jesus never hesitated to tell his followers that he wanted all or nothing. Indeed, Jesus said that their love for him needed to be so great that all other human relationships would pale by comparison. While only Jesus qualifies for that kind of devotion, we can learn from this passage that skilled leaders don't blink when urging others to count the cost. They know that no follower who has a half-hearted commitment will ever become a leader.*

Jesus didn't set a timeframe for length of service. His team understood they would serve indefinitely—and so they did. Not everyone could be Jesus' disciple. Jesus rejected the rich ruler's offer of service, even though he probably would have donated money to Jesus' ministry. Jesus didn't want his wealth if He didn't have his whole heart.

You might be thinking: *Women won't make that kind of a commitment.* You're partially right; everyone won't, but you don't need everyone. You just need six to eight (three to four) dedicated servants who understand and embrace the cost of following in Jesus' footsteps, and will in turn, find six to eight (three to four) dedicated servants to serve on their teams.

You're not asking a woman to give up *everything* to serve, but some may feel that their time is too big a sacrifice and, like the rich ruler, they'll miss the blessing of serving with Jesus. Notice I said serving with and not for Jesus. Jesus doesn't need us; we need Him. He could get His work done without us—we're not essential to His plan—but He is essential to us becoming women worthy of being followers of Christ.

Customize

BUILDING: Recruit shepherd coaches willing to make this their main area of service and lead indefinitely. Don't minimize the cost or lure them with a short-term service commitment. Discuss that you don't want them stretched too thin and a shepherd coach position is a key leadership role. Understandably, in smaller churches, women often wear several hats.

REMODELING: If you haven't previously asked team members to serve long-term or to make this their main area of service, start now. Ask current shepherd coaches for a commitment to support the reorganization process. For those who can't or won't commit, meet with them to find out what's going on in their lives and listen to their concerns. They may prefer serving on a team rather than leading one. Let them make that change gracefully.

REFURBISHING: If the team has served with you for a significant period of time, you understand the value of a team growing and learning together. Constant changes in leadership cause disruption and lack of continuity. However, new blood also infuses new ideas. If someone on the team is ready to retire or move on, help her find and train a replacement, and then let her go.

Tools

Love Me with Stubborn Love by Anne Ortlund

The Purpose Driven Life by Rick Warren

Face-to-Face with Aquila and Priscilla: Balancing Life and Ministry by Janet Thompson

Less Is More Leadership: 8 Secrets to How to Lead and Still Have a Life by H. Dale Burke

Awaken the Leader in You: 10 Essentials for Women in Leadership by Linda M. Clark

Team-Building Project

As Christian leaders, our responsibility is to educate team members in how to prioritize life so there's *always* time to serve the Lord. That means we need to know how to do this ourselves. A biblical way to keep your life in step with God is by following His priorities and helping the team learn to do the same. Lead a discussion on prioritizing and balancing life that incorporates the following points:

1. Priority One—Jesus at the center of your life. Serving doesn't equal loving, but you must love Jesus before you can serve Him, then nothing except you

can stop God from working in and through you. If you're too busy to serve the Lord, you're too busy. We often use time as an excuse not to be about the Lord's work, but consider standing in front of Jesus Christ saying, "Sorry, Lord, I have so many things to do, I can't serve You. I'm just too busy." That provides a different perspective, doesn't it?

2. Priority Two — The family of God, which encompasses your family (Matthew 12:48-50). Your community of fellow believers is your extended family. *"As for me and my house, we will serve the Lord"* (Joshua 24:15 NKJV).

3. Priority Three — Evangelism of the world Christ died for — the unbelievers (Matthew 28:16–20). How we live according to Priorities 1 and 2 determines the effectiveness of our witness and service to achieve the ultimate purpose of ministry: furthering God's kingdom.

Take this quiz with the team:

1. Where might God be asking you to sacrifice more than you have already?
2. What "gods" in your life need to be eliminated?
3. Where are you putting the world's work before God's work?
4. Rate yourself in the three priorities of life. If you're off balance, what changes can you make so God can use you to your fullest potential?
5. When making a time and money investment, ask: Will this outlive me for the glory of God?
6. How can team members help each other maintain the three priorities?

Help the team see areas where they're substituting the world's priorities for God's priorities. Guide them in turning their focus back to God by dying to themselves and living for Christ (1 Corinthians 15:31). There is no better way.

Leader to Leader

I'm sure I wasn't God's first choice to start a global mentoring movement among churches, but I was the person who said, "OK, I'll go wherever You ask and do whatever You want." God took a willing, committed heart and made me into a woman worthy of being a servant leader of Jesus Christ. He did that for you, too, when you willingly laid down your current life and took up the glorious life He had planned for you in leadership. That's the message you need to share with your team.

When I received the "Feed my sheep" call from the Lord, Jesus tested the willingness of my husband and me to sacrifice to serve Him. I was managing a branch of an insurance agency and attending seminary at night and on the weekends. Eight months later, my manager told me he was demoting me because he didn't feel the company was number one in my life. I agreed with him that my priorities were God, family, and work, but that hadn't altered my job performance. He responded that the company needed to be god in my life—my "religion."

It was as if Jesus was standing behind my manager's chair reminding me that I couldn't serve two masters. I had to make a choice. I quit that high-paying career to go into full-time lay ministry and follow "God's call," which wasn't too big a sacrifice since my husband had a lucrative career. Within three months of quitting my job and starting the Woman to Woman Mentoring Ministry, my husband was laid off in a corporate downsizing and was out of work for eighteen months.

That was a *huge* turning point and challenge for us. Would we stay faithful to the call the Lord had so clearly put on my life, when *logically* I should quit the "volunteer" ministry and find paying work during my husband's unemployment? We're glad we didn't make the latter choice. We wouldn't exchange anything for the blessing of watching lives change through the Woman to Woman Mentoring Ministry, and About His Work, my writing and speaking ministry which God developed during our faith-testing time.

My husband and I trust that God has a plan when we make ourselves available. We don't try to outguess God; we follow His lead, which usually involves sacrifice. I didn't tell you our story to pat myself on the back or imply that you're going to lose your job or have to give up everything to serve God. But would it be so bad if you did? Could you trust completely in God to provide if you knew you were doing exactly what He wanted you to do? Faith is believing in things we don't see (2 Corinthians 5:7), and while it may not look possible to your eyes and mind, you'll miss seeing many of God's miracles of provision if you're always trying to figure things out yourself.

As the ministry visionary director, you set the pace for the team and ministry: not as a martyr but in lifestyle. Your sacrifices to do God's work and the fruit and blessings from your labor of love provide the team with an example of commitment and service.

Finishing Touches

- A woman with an unbelieving and/or unsupportive husband will find it difficult, if not impossible, to serve effectively in a leadership role. She may be passionate about her service and willing to make the sacrifice to serve as a leader, but if her husband isn't supportive of the ministry work requirements or doesn't understand the Jesus his wife serves, it causes undue stress at home and the woman won't be able to keep her ministry commitments.

  I didn't initially understand this phenomenon. In one particular interview, I asked if the woman had talked about the service opportunity with her unbelieving husband, and if he knew the demands of the role. The response was, "Yes, he said I could do it." Then, she wasn't able to come to required meetings, couldn't serve in the evening or on weekends, and so it went. She couldn't fulfill the leadership responsibilities because her husband wasn't willing to endure the cost. It put unnecessary pressure on the marriage, and that isn't the way to win a spouse to the Lord. You want these precious "spiritually-single" women to feel included, so find less demanding and short-term places for them to serve as helpers on a team.

- When interviewing for a leadership position, use the Interview Questionnaire on page 60 to determine if:
  - the husband is a believer.
  - she's willing to commit to a long-term role in the ministry.
  - she will make this her primary ministry service, with the understanding that in a smaller church she may need to perform several roles.

~ Use the "Duration" section of the Service Opportunity Description (chap. 14, p. 99) to discuss the expectations of a shepherd coach. Provide a three-month trial period before asking for a long-term commitment. This allows both of you to see if the position is a good fit.

~ I often hear of recruiting leaders for only one year of service, but you'll never have a team of committed dedicated leaders if you follow that philosophy. Leading takes focus, and it takes years to nurture a leader. For longevity, consistency, and loyalty, select women who are willing to accept the cost of following you as you follow Jesus (1 Corinthians 11:1).

Mentoring Moment

Don't sacrifice God's work; sacrifice to do God's work.

Jesus Was Specific About the Job Requirements

These were his instructions.

—MARK 6:8

The Cornerstone

In Mark 6:8–11, Jesus gave team members instructions for accomplishing their assigned job. Matthew 10:5 to 11:1 elaborates on these instructions. Jesus specified His expectations and the job requirements. Mark 14:13*b*–15 is another example of Jesus instructing two of His team members in how to find the house for the Passover meal.

The Blueprint

In chapter 7, we discussed the Service Opportunity Description. This is a vital part of the initial interview, providing the prospective team member with pertinent information regarding the position and the expectations and requirements to fulfill the role. This is similar to a job description and clearly explains the ministry or leadership position:

- Purpose
- Requirements
- Responsibilities
- Duration

Customize

BUILDING: Write a Service Opportunity Description for each of the six to eight (four to eight) shepherd coach positions using the format and example in "Tools," the tips in the "Team-Building Project," and the purpose statements you wrote in chapter 11, p. 79. Use these in interviewing prospective team members (see chapter 7, pages 59–63). Help the shepherd coaches write Service Opportunity Descriptions for the team leaders they will recruit, who will in turn write them for their prospective coordinators and helpers.

REMODELING: Perhaps there hasn't been a clear understanding in the past of each team member's role and job responsibilities. Ask each shepherd coach to write a Service Opportunity Description for her position and then review it with her. Use this as an opportunity to clarify any misunderstandings and expectations. Next, have the shepherd coaches write Service Opportunity Descriptions for their prospective team leaders, who will then write them for their prospective coordinators, who will then write them for their prospective helpers.

REFURBISHING: Follow the steps in "Remodeling." Again, if this is a new concept, the shepherd coaches may not think they need Service Opportunity Descriptions. Emphasize the benefits to their teams, who will serve more efficiently and effectively.

Tools

See the sample Service Opportunity Description to customize on the following page.

Service Opportunity Description for: *(Fill in position.)*

Your Shepherd: *(Fill in name and position of the person she reports to.)*

Purpose: *(For the position—one-sentence statement.)*

Service Requirements: *(List specific times and places where she would need to be present.)*

-
-
-
-

Service Responsibilities: *(Overview of what the position entails.)*

1.

2.

3.

4.

5.

6.

7.

8.

9.

10.

Service Duration: *(Indicate long-term commitment for leadership—could be one year for helpers. Request finding a replacement before leaving.)*

If you agree, please sign and date:_____
(Select an appropriate Scripture.)

Sample Shepherd Coach Service Opportunity Description

ANYWHERE CHURCH WOMEN'S MINISTRY

Service Opportunity Description for: *Special Events Shepherd Coach*
Your Shepherd: *Ministry Visionary Director*

Purpose: To develop, train, equip, and oversee a team that provides opportunities for fun, fellowship, spiritual growth, and learning for the women of Anywhere Church and the community.

Service Requirements
- Must love to have fun and enjoy hospitality.
- Event planning experience is helpful, but not required.
- Organized and flexible.
- Creative and willing to think beyond what seems possible.
- Access to computer and email.
- Recruit and train an apprentice.
- Serve on the administrative team and attend meetings, miniretreats, and planning retreats.
- Willing to make this your focused area of ministry.

Service Responsibilities:
1. Develop and lead special events team leaders and assist them in building their teams.
2. Plan and execute the event program and calendar for women's ministry.
3. Work with financial shepherd coach to establish a budget and obtain required funds.
4. Consult with outreach shepherd coach for outreach events.
5. Coordinate with other shepherd coaches as needed.
6. Meet monthly with special events team leaders.

Service Duration:
A shepherd coach position is a long-term and committed role, so the first three months is a time to determine if this is a good fit for you and the ministry. If you continue on as shepherd coach, we ask that you train a replacement before vacating the position.
If you agree, please sign and date:_____

Let's have a feast and celebrate.   — LUKE 15:23

Team-Building Project

If you're building a team, you'll need Service Opportunity Descriptions for each shepherd coach position so you can start interviewing. If you're remodeling or refurbishing, set realistic timeframes for the shepherd coaches to write their sService Opportunity Descriptions and provide sessions for the team to work together.

Guidelines and ideas for writing Service Opportunity Descriptions:

1. Review this chapter.
2. Each position on the team needs a Service Opportunity Description.
3. Be specific with the requirements, expectations, duration, and commitment of the position.
4. Provide a summary (not extensive details) that fits on one page.
5. Revise when there are changes to the position's responsibilities.
6. Standardize throughout the ministry.

Tips for shepherd coaches writing a Service Opportunity Description for their own position:

1. Remember the purpose of your position is to develop a team, not to do all the work yourself.
2. Write down the gifts, talents, and capabilities you bring to the position. God has gifted you with certain spiritual gifts and personality traits pertinent to being a shepherd coach in your area. What are they?
3. What is the scope of your area? What tasks does it entail?
4. What do you need to know to be a shepherd coach for your area? For example, someone who doesn't know how to play soccer couldn't be a soccer coach, even if she was a great leader. You don't teach a coach how to play soccer: she knows and excels at soccer before becoming a coach.
5. Have another team member read and review your Service Opportunity Description to see if it is clear and understandable.
6. Review with the ministry visionary director.

Leader to Leader

Few people accept a new job without knowing the expectations and requirements of the job. Similarly in ministry, every woman should know in advance whether she could fulfill the responsibilities of a position, and she should receive guidance in performing the role successfully. It's easy to forget something when you're interviewing someone, and there's the temptation to talk her into a position or "strategically" leave something out.

Service Opportunity Descriptions keep you both on track and focused, providing a tangible information tool for discussion. The prospective team member can take it home and pray over the responsibilities before accepting the position. Later, she can use it to guide her as she performs the duties of the position.

If you're remodeling or refurbishing a team, having the shepherd coaches write their own descriptions gives you insight into how they see their roles. It also gives you the opportunity to review with them any changes or modifications you would like to make.

You may choose to call the Service Opportunity Descriptions something different, but using the suggested format saves you valuable time redesigning one.

Finishing Touches

- During an interview, Service Opportunity Descriptions help you remember what the job entails, and the person considering the position doesn't have to remember everything you said.
- Both parties know the job requirements and responsibilities. For example: Someone offering to help the hospitality coordinator with registration discovers on the registrar's Service Opportunity Description that she needs to arrive an hour before the event, but she won't be off work in time. Better to know this in advance than the morning of the event. Maybe she could serve on the cleanup team instead. Then the coordinator can continue looking for someone who can fulfill the registrar's responsibilities.

Mentoring Moment

Service Opportunity Descriptions help with communication, clarification, and commitment.

CHAPTER 15

Jesus Cast His Vision

Jesus said to Simon, "Don't be afraid; from now on you will catch men." So they pulled their boats up on shore, left everything and followed him.

—LUKE 5:10–11

Jesus went out and saw a tax collector by the name of Levi sitting at his tax booth. "Follow me," Jesus said to him, and Levi got up, left everything and followed him.

—LUKE 5:27–28

The Cornerstone

Jesus was a visionary who boldly and effectively proclaimed the plans He had for His team. Jesus was going to heal, preach, teach, cast out demons, and evangelize the world, and He invited His team to join Him in that grand and glorious purpose. Those He called were so impressed with His vision that they left their professions and livelihoods to join His team.

The Blueprint

Before you develop a team, you must know where you're taking them. You need to verbalize your ministry goals and vision to the team and update them frequently. Most importantly, you solicit the team's support and excitement for the vision. In order for team members to support and embrace a vision, they must take ownership. Then *your* vision transforms to *their* vision: a universal ministry vision.

You'll present two categories of visions and goals: long range and short range. Long-range visions may be immensely far-reaching and seem impossible; short-range goals are specific, measurable, and lead to accomplishing the bigger visions. You can't have one without the other—without a long-range vision your short range-goals will be scattered and become more problem-solving solutions than goals. Without short-range goals supporting your long-range vision, the vision will be an unattainable dream.

Customize

BUILDING: Accepting or aspiring to leadership encompasses a vision. As you considered the ministry visionary director position, you thought about what it would look like to be in this leadership role. You pictured what you wanted to accomplish and where you would take the ministry in the future. Those were visualizations and goals that need to be shared with prospective team members.

REMODELING: What are your visions and goals for restructuring the team? If you're assuming leadership from a predecessor, no matter how successful the previous leader, you come in with fresh new ideas and a vision of the ministry and the team with you at the helm. What changes will that require? Share the answers to these questions with your current team members and solicit their support for your plans.

REFURBISHING: Maybe it's time to establish a new vision. It's easy to keep the status quo and get into a rut over the years. Ask the team to brainstorm with you new ideas and ways of doing things that will enhance and rejuvenate the ministry. Think big!

Tools

Here's an example of a vision and goal statement I shared with the team.

ANNUAL VISION AND GOALS

Long-Range Vision

1. Every shepherd coach would have an apprentice and team leaders.
2. We would be part of Saddleback's Global P.E.A.C.E. Plan by sharing Woman to Woman Mentoring with the world.
3. We would continue to seek ways to bring unity and closeness into our relationships, thereby living out our ministry verse, Titus 2:3–5.
4. We would remember it's not about us, but instead how God is using us to change lives one woman at a time, fulfilling the initial call to "Feed my sheep."
5. Living, loving, laughing . . . working, worshipping, witnessing the wonders we have seen the Lord do in our life and ministry.

Short-Range Goals

1. We would complete our team with a prayer chain shepherd coach and financial shepherd coach.
2. We would continue to develop more avenues for involving ministry members by providing them opportunities to serve in the ministry.
3. Each shepherd coach would have monthly meetings and a Christmas party for her team.
4. Our focus would be the heart of each individual woman who joins the ministry . . . not worrying about numbers, but resting in the assurance that God does the bringing, we just need to be available to do the serving.
5. Pursue new avenues of publicizing the ministry, especially to the mature believing women of our church.

Team-Building Project

You might be asking yourself: How do I come up with a vision? Read what Richard and Henry Blackaby say about vision casting in *Spiritual Leadership*:

If Jesus provides the model for spiritual leadership, then the key is not for leaders to develop visions and to set the direction for their organizations. The key is to obey and to preserve everything the Father reveals to them of his will. Ultimately, the Father is the leader. God has the vision of what he wants to do. God does not ask leaders to dream big dreams for him or to solve the problems that confront them. He asks leaders to walk with him so intimately that, when he reveals what is on his agenda, they will immediately adjust their lives to his will and the results will bring glory to God.

For a vision-casting and goal-setting exercise, try the following:

1. Get away to a quiet place and worship in solitude with the Lord. Pray for God to give you a vision for what He wants to accomplish in and through the ministry. Let your team members know when you will be on this prayer quest and ask them to be in prayer also.

2. Write down the ministry visions and goals God reveals to you without considering whether they're doable or possible. Think: no restrictions.

3. Review the items on your list, see them in your mind, dream about them from your heart, and pray over them with your soul.

4. Cast out fear. Fear is from Satan, not from God. Fear is based on worrying about: *What if I fail? What will others think? Are these visions and ideas foolish? Are they doable?* If God is behind your vision, you can trust and have faith that nothing is too big for Him, or He will replace your vision with one that fits His plans.

5. Visions may be hard to describe—they may be more a sense of something possible in the future but not tangible at the moment. Do the best you can to put it into words.

6. Goals are specific, attainable, realistic, and measurable. They are not just things you're going to "try" to do, but things you know are accomplishable with effort, energy, and passion.

7. Categorize your list into long-range visions that might take years to accomplish and short-range goals that are doable in a year and support the long-range visions. Then: *"Commit to the Lord whatever you do, and your plans will succeed"* (Proverbs 16:3).

8. Share your visions and goals with your current team and each new team member you recruit.

Leader to *Leader*

I encourage you to adopt a title such as *ministry visionary director* that places your role in proper perspective and accomplishes two important objectives:

1. *Visionary* conveys openness to the great and grand things the Lord is going to do in the ministry. *Director* conveys overseeing the team's role in following and supporting the vision. This prevents the ministry from centering on one person and puts the emphasis on teamwork.

2. Visionaries establish the atmosphere of future change—growth, mobility, maturity, improvement, new ideas, reaching out above and beyond what we think we can do, and stretching. Life will never be static with a visionary on the team.

At your administrative team planning retreat (see chap. 22), cast the visions and goals you feel God has revealed to you for the upcoming year. Ask the shepherd coaches to share their visions and plans for their teams. Pray that the Lord will give you clarity and insight as to what He wants you doing in the future. Discuss and pray about whether these visions and goals seem achievable. Once you arrive at a mutually agreeable and prayed-over list, write out the ministry visions and goals for the upcoming year and give each team member a copy. Encourage them to do the same for their visions of where God wants to take their teams in the upcoming year and years.

Then pray that the team will enthusiastically and passionately embrace your visions and goals. Otherwise, nothing happens. One unsupportive team member can sabotage even the best thought-out plans. The key to implementation is having *all* team members on board. It's important to entertain questions and discussion. If someone isn't comfortable with a vision or goal, don't ignore her feelings. It could be a misunderstanding or misperception. You'll need to spend extra time with her, talking and praying together until she trusts the plans and you can trust that she'll do her best to fulfill them.

I'm known for my passion for mentoring, and that fuels my ministry service. But nothing excites me more then to hear a team member express her own passion for a goal or vision, and I know this fuels her service.

Finishing Touches

∼ Study the effectiveness of Jesus' vision casting with His team. What can you learn for your own vision casting? Here are some points to consider:

∼∼ Jesus started His ministry before calling the disciples, therefore, establishing credibility — *"News about him spread through the whole countryside"* (Luke 4:14). When they joined Him, the team knew of His incredible work and vision.

∼∼ Jesus told His team they would be doing something bigger than themselves — something only God could do in and through them.

∼∼ Jesus spoke their language. To the fishermen He talked of fishing for men, not global evangelism — a foreign term to them at the time. Fishing they understood, and every fisherman is a visionary. Fishermen never set out on a fishing trip expecting to catch nothing, even though that's a real possibility. They envision themselves with the big catch, and they keep fishing expectantly.

∼∼ Jesus told them not to be afraid — He had a plan and He would equip and train them to be part of it.

∼ Learning from Jesus:

∼∼ Follow your vision of building, remodeling, or refurbishing the ministry, as we talked about in chapter 5. Let others see that you're dedicated to the vision and to making it a reality.

∼∼ As you recruit and develop the team, share your vision and goals with them. Passion is contagious. If you want them to become excited, you must be excited.

∼∼ When introducing a new idea or vision, admit there might be hindrances. However, also explain that if it was doable, you would limit God to your capabilities, and you want the ministry based on God's capabilities.

∼∼ Speak the language of team members. To what will the women relate?

New ideas and change can be scary, and there will be those who readily tell you something isn't going to work. A wise leader acknowledges and doesn't make light of those concerns. Usually fear is at the heart of hesitancy. Assure the team members that you'll work beside them and entertain their ideas for implementation.

It's essential that the team trusts God and trusts you as a godly person of prayer. Even if they have misgivings, you need to be able to trust that they'll not undermine you or the plans God has given you. It will be much harder if you don't solicit their loyalty. Not impossible: Judas' treachery didn't stop Jesus from accomplishing what He came to do.

Dissension and resistance can become a crippling cancer in the ministry. If a team member isn't in agreement with the team plans, don't ignore her feelings. Take her aside and address her concerns. She may have some good points you hadn't considered. Ask her to give the new ideas and visions a try, assuring her you want the best for the ministry. Read chapter 21 for more ideas on how to handle this situation.

We often limit our ministries to what we logically think is accomplishable, and our team follows our lead. As Christians, we're not limited to our own capabilities. If God is in it, it will be bigger than what we think we can do. We need to challenge our teams and ourselves to do the impossible, because with God everything is possible (Mark 10:27). When the impossible becomes possible, God gets all the glory.

Don't put God's plans and visions for the ministry into the small box of your mind: Let your vision expand to God's size. Think big!

Remain open to what it seems only God can do, and then you have a vision.

A visionary asks: "What could we attempt to do if we weren't worried about failing?" Visionaries are willing to take the risk of failure.

Mentoring Moment

"Today's impossible problem is tomorrow's miracle." — Rick Warren

Maturing, Equipping, and Commissioning the Team

Jesus Trained His Team

One day Jesus was praying in a certain place. When he finished, one of his disciples said to him, "Lord, teach us to pray, just as John taught his disciples." He said to them, "When you pray say: 'Father, hallowed be your name, your kingdom come.'"

— LUKE 11:1–2

The Cornerstone

Throughout the Gospels, we observe Jesus answering questions, teaching, and performing miracles in front of the disciples. They didn't usually understand what Jesus was doing, but He was patient and persistent, often stopping to explain the meaning or purpose behind His actions or comments. Jesus utilized a variety of training methods:

- Jesus had His team accompany Him to observe and learn while He taught and ministered (Mark 1:16–45; 2:1–12; 5:1–43; 8:22–26).
- Jesus allowed His team to ask questions (Mark 4:10; 7:17; 9:11–13; 10:10–12, 26–27; 13:3–4).
- Jesus asked them questions (Mark 7:18; 8:17–21, 27–30; 9:33; 10:38).
- Jesus was the master at "situational training": The use of spontaneous situations to teach, train, and explain (Mark 2:15 to 3:6; 4:1–34; 7:1–23; 10:1–34; 11:12–26; 12:41–44; 13:28–31).
- Jesus picked an "inner core" of three disciples to receive advanced

training and participate in unique and private circumstances (Mark 5:37–43; 9:2–13; 14:32–41).

- Jesus assured His team they had the power to do everything they saw Him doing (Mark 16:15–20). He didn't make them feel inferior by insinuating He could perform tasks better and faster than them, and He didn't step in and do their work.

- Jesus used their disappointments as a teaching opportunity (Mark 9:14–29).

The Blueprint

You never "arrive" as a leader: Leadership is an ongoing process of studying, learning, and mentoring. Every leader is a reader. The same applies to team members, who will be the future leaders of the ministry and building their own teams. We all learn differently, so it's important to offer a variety of teaching modes and use every situation as a training opportunity.

Jesus consistently worked Himself out of an earthly job. From the beginning of His ministry, He equipped His team to replace Him. Jesus understood that He must decrease so that they could increase because soon He would be gone and they would have to carry on without His physical presence. He wanted them to succeed. The closer He got to the cross, the more Jesus trained His team.

Customize

BUILDING: New team members will need training. Focus on the most essential tasks first and utilize situational opportunities as they arise. Don't overload them with information. When you add a team member, provide her with tools you've given the team. Assign a mentor from the team to give her previous training information and walk beside her as she finds her place on the team.

REMODELING: Are there shepherd coaches who could help you implement some of the new or revised projects and procedures? Have you identified an "inner core"? Change is difficult, so having someone from within the team assist you in introducing new ideas will help the team's receptiveness. Have prospective co-trainers read this section in the book and utilize their ideas and skills.

REFURBISHING: The team may have mastered their current tasks and be ready to tackle new challenges. You should have identified an "inner core" of two or three shepherd coaches who could assist you in taking the team to the next level spiritually and practically. If possible, let the "core" do all the training, while you observe.

Tools

Suggested books for the team to read and discuss during trainings:

The Team That Jesus Built by Janet Thompson

Leadership Above the Line by Dr. Sarah Sumner

On Being a Servant of God by Warren W. Wiersbe

Spiritual Leadership by Henry and Richard Blackaby

The Secret by Ken Blanchard

Women Leading Women by Jaye Martin and Terri Stovall

The Leadership Bible: Leadership Principles from God's Word (Zondervan)

Select only books, media, conferences, and seminars that teach Christian leadership principles. Teams are transitional and books can become costly, so determine which books are personal growth books they can keep if they leave the team and which books will be "ministry-owned" and passed on to their successor.

Team-Building Project

I'm known for stretching people, and Jesus surely did His share of stretching people as well. During one training session, I gave everyone rubber bands. When they felt that I was introducing an "out-there" concept, they snapped their rubber band to remember—a rubber band's purpose is to be stretched.

Training Activity Depicting the Value of Teamwork

In the "refurbishing" stage of our team, I invited several team members to create an exercise that depicted the value of teamwork. They designed, implemented, and led the training on applying the principles derived from the following activity. Let the team use their creativity to help you plan similar training exercises. In this exercise, the training is not about how to construct a book, it's about being more efficient and productive as a team.

1. Set up four work stations with supplies and tools to make paper booklets.
2. Construct an example of a finished booklet for them to duplicate. You can make the booklet as simple or intricate as you choose.
3. Split the team into workforces of one-, two-, three-, and four-person groups, depending on the size of the team, and give them a time limit to see how many booklets each team can construct.

TRAINING PRINCIPLE: The teams with more than one member must organize and communicate so that team members use their strengths to systematically work together for the common goal. The team with only one member may have perfect booklets, but production is minimal and the work is lonely.

After completing this exercise, the team readily saw the importance of working on all ministry projects as a team. This concept was further emphasized and embraced by the fact that fellow team members designed the project. The training point evolved from within the team, rather than being taught to them.

Leader to Leader

Each year I based training projects and materials on the theme God gave me for our annual fall planning retreat. You might look at the list under "Tools" in this chapter and decide the team needs every suggested book right now! They probably do, but not all at once. Select materials that support your current focus and give the team time to absorb and apply the information before moving on to the next resource. Occasionally, the team pleaded with me, "Please no more books for a while!"

Provide formal trainings several times a year, but also be alert to teaching opportunities in the routine ministry operations—situational training. When problems arise, if time allows, let the team work on a solution. They may arrive at the appropriate conclusion or you may need to guide them, but don't solve the problem for them. The most effective training is your role modeling and helping them find a pearl of wisdom from the various situations that arise daily in ministry—most people learn best by observing and then doing.

If a situation requires an immediate response, lead them through the solution while explaining your actions and letting them know they'll be able to handle a similar situation next time.

Finishing Touches

Here's an example of a situational training opportunity that occurred in our ministry. The problem: We ran out of chairs at an event held at a home. I asked the team to consider how to prevent this happening in the future. Some of their solutions were . . .

- Limit attendance to the number of chairs.
- When we run out of chairs, close the door.
- Buy more chairs.
- Have someone who lives nearby be "on call" to bring more chairs.
- Store extra folding chairs in the garage of the home.
- Have each team member bring chairs to the event.

The first step was to make sure everyone shared the same philosophy and goals as we talked through suggested solutions. We went back to our mission statement which states that *Saddleback women of all ages are welcome to our event*. Therefore, we determined: We would never turn someone away because we couldn't find her a chair.

Now with all in agreement of the common goal, we could discuss solutions that supported that goal. So we brainstormed:

- If necessary, women could sit on the floor or the stairs.
- If we bought more chairs, we'd have to find a place to store them between events.

⮴ "On-call chair suppliers" create an urgent, panic-filled atmosphere we wanted to avoid.

⮴ We didn't want team members to have to worry about bringing chairs on event day.

SOLUTION: Buy more chairs to store with permission at the event location.

Helping the team work through a suitable strategy teaches problem-solving skills that support the ministry goals and can apply to other areas. However, remember that the apostles never stopped asking questions and usually didn't understand Jesus' explanations or situational training, but He didn't give up. When He was gone, they knew how to get the job done.

A secure leader isn't threatened by talent on her team—she embraces it. Provide opportunities for team members to excel. Encourage the women to use their gifts and teach them how to lead out of their strengths. Remember: You're training the team to replace you—to function in your absence.

Mentoring Moment

"A leader attracts people to a cause and holds them with the power of his or her teaching. Only lessons well learned and fully internalized hold followers for the long pull; it is only these lessons that keep followers faithful and committed when the inevitable tough times come."

—BOB BRINER AND RAY PRITCHARD, *Leadership Lessons of Jesus*

Jesus Wasn't Discouraged When His Team Made Mistakes

After Jesus had gone indoors, his disciples asked him privately, "Why couldn't we drive it [a demon] out?" He replied, "This kind can come out only by prayer."
— MARK 9:28–29

The Cornerstone

Initially, the apostles weren't skilled in ministry. They became more effective after Jesus left the ministry to them and ascended back to heaven, leaving the Holy Spirit to guide and direct them. Even when they bumbled and questioned Jesus to the point of seeming not to believe in His vision, He didn't lose heart. He didn't give up on them. He continued to patiently and deliberately teach, train, and release them. Jesus helped His team see where they needed improvement, and then, sent them out again.

The Blueprint

Team members are going to make mistakes—maybe even big ones. You have a choice: Make them feel like failures or . . .

- ➣ Applaud what they did right.
- ➣ Ask where they see need for improvement.
- ➣ Point out areas you notice that need changing.

➣ Discuss a new plan.
➣ Send them out to try again.
➣ Pray for their success.

Customize

BUILDING: As the new team ventures out to lead their own teams, they're going to make mistakes. Extend grace, ask questions, offer suggestions without pointing fingers or condemning, and commend them for taking the initiative. Don't rush in and fix the situation, berate them, or take the task back. Brainstorm together changes or new strategies, pray, and send them back out.

REMODELING: You may feel you're at the remodeling stage because of the many mistakes the team has made, or perhaps, you didn't have patience with them when they fumbled. Maybe some team members didn't take their positions seriously. Whatever the reasons, you're taking the initiative to regroup now, and I commend you for not giving up. I hope I've given you tools in this book to complete your remodeling, and now, I'm sending you out to do just that!

REFURBISHING: As you share new ideas from this book with the team, some will make mistakes and not everyone will follow the plan exactly. That's OK; they're trying. Your role is encouraging your shepherd coaches to try the new steps with their teams and not become discouraged if everything doesn't go "by the book." You have a perfect opportunity to create the team that Jesus built. You go, girl!

Tools

Tips for Managing Mistakes

➣ Shepherds make sure their sheep stay on the right path. You may need to step in occasionally to get a shepherd coach back on the right path after she has strayed, and she may need to do the same with her team members. Once they are all back on their feet and headed in the right direction, however, the shepherd keeps an eye on them from a safe distance.

Don't jump in and do a team member's job when she fumbles. When a team player fumbles during a ball game, the coach doesn't run down on the field, grab the ball from the player's hand, and complete the play. Players make mistakes and they might lose a few games, but the coach stays where he or she can look at the big picture, help and nurture the other players, and provide direction and guidance to the entire team. Coaches demonstrate their expertise during practice and training, but they could never singlehandedly match a unified team. If the coach is *running* the plays, the team is going to lose anyway for lack of a leader *calling* the plays.

This strategy applies to you too—if you're constantly doing theshepherd coach's job, you can't be the ministry visionary director, and if the shepherd coaches aren't developing capable teams, they can't be shepherd coaches.

Learning takes place when we make mistakes, so don't always prevent mistakes unless a mistake would be detrimental to a team member or the ministry.

Let the team experience disappointments and assure them they're still worthy as leaders. Ask what they learned, mentor them with your wisdom, and send them back into the ministry field.

Guide and correct without chastising. Everyone makes mistakes, but it's the wise person who doesn't make the same mistake twice.

Team-Building Project

1. Identify an area you've held onto because you're fearful someone else wouldn't do it right.
2. Now, think of a team member you could delegate, equip, and empower to do this task.
3. Go through "Empowerment Steps" with her (chap. 23, pages 169–170).
4. If mistakes or problems occur, determine if they're minor and can be overlooked or important enough for you to address.
5. If you're sure the mistakes are in the latter category, go through "The Blueprint" steps in this chapter. Jesus did, and you can too!
6. When she's ready, let go and let her assume responsibility for the task.

Leader to Leader

Dealing with mistakes wasn't an easy step for me. As the originator of the mentoring ministry, I had a sense of how things should be done and that others probably wouldn't do everything "the right way." In the beginning of the letting-go process, I wanted to double check everything.

Often, a team member would ask for my input when venturing into new territory on her own, but sometimes she didn't. As you might expect, there were fumbles. However, allowing the team to learn from experience and consequences are invaluable lessons, even when every bone in your body wants to bail them out. I can't say I resisted interfering in the beginning, but as we all realized that mistakes were usually fixable, I relaxed and they started making fewer mistakes. I also prayed for them to make the right decisions and to be successful. I wanted them to succeed.

When I first started the mentoring ministry, I did every position myself. As I began recruiting, training, and passing on much of the work, one area I held onto the longest was the Prayer Day Matching. That's the day for matching mentors with mentees through intercessory prayer. I created that day, wrote the guidelines, have the gift of discernment for matching—I was certain the matching couldn't be done effectively without me. I couldn't let go. Then one day the Lord reminded me that churches around the world were having Matching Prayer Days without me, and they were doing just fine. What made me think I was so important that the Prayer Day shepherd coach and her team couldn't do it without me?

That was a wake-up call. I didn't back out of Prayer Day immediately, but instead practiced Empowerment Steps described in chapter 23, pages 169–170.

- I participated in Prayer Day with them.
- I then started coming later in the day after they had started praying and matching.
- I progressed to just checking in at lunchtime.
- It wasn't long before I wasn't part of the day at all, and they faxed me the final matches.
- Eventually, I didn't see the final matches.

Yes, they made some questionable matches, but they learned for the next time.

Finishing Touches

- For a visual of this chapter, consider the process of children learning independence. They fall down often when they're learning to walk and they miss their mouth trying to feed themselves, but if we carry them or continue spoon-feeding them, we would be doing that for the rest of their lives and ours!

- We also don't chastise toddlers when they fall down or when they hit their eye instead of their mouth with their spoon. We encourage them for trying, provide a few pointers, and let them do it again under our watchful eye.

- Soon they're walking and eating without us even in the room. If they walk into a table or drop food on their clothes, we don't get discouraged. We pick them up or brush them off and cheer them on to try again.

- We don't tell children how we can walk and feed ourselves better than them or start doing everything for them again.

- Parents succeed in parenting when a child can function on his or her own.

- This doesn't happen overnight with children, and it won't with the team either.

- Whether you've built, remodeled, or refurbished, you've birthed a new team and they're learning new ways of leading. Allow sufficient time and don't become impatient with the process, or you'll find them continuing to defer to you or maybe even quitting for fear they'll let you down.

Mentoring Moment

Every leader's ultimate goal should be to decrease while the team increases.

Jesus Sent Out His Team in Pairs

Calling the Twelve to him, he sent them out two by two and gave them authority over evil spirits.

— MARK 6:7

So he sent two of his disciples.

— MARK 14:13

The Cornerstone

Solomon gave wise advice in Ecclesiastes 4:9–12: "*Two are better than one, because they have a good return for their work: If one falls down, his friend can help him up. But pity the man who falls and has no one to help him up!*" Mark 6:12–13 confirms this was an effective approach. When Jesus sent the disciples two by two, "*They went out and preached that people should repent. They drove out many demons and anointed many sick people with oil and healed them.*" In another instance "*The Lord appointed seventy-two others and sent them two by two ahead of him to every town and place where he was about to go*" (Luke 10:1).

The Blueprint

Every position in the ministry should follow Jesus' example of "*two by two*" and have an apprentice, starting with the ministry visionary director and the administrative team. On the team charts in the appendix, the ministry visionary directors, shepherd coaches, team leaders, and coordinators have apprentices. There's always a replacement trained and ready to fill in an emergency, or when someone moves, gets sick, or stops serving for whatever reason.

Apprentices learn by assisting the person to whom they are apprentices. They're ready to step in and take those women's places if and when necessary. With this *two by two* method, team members don't experience burnout because they're sharing the workload. If a team member vacates a position, there's no gap in service: someone trained and ready steps into the position.

Customize

BUILDING: Develop your "core" of two or three shepherd coaches who excel in leadership skills. Pray for one to emerge as your apprentice. Assist all shepherd coaches in writing an apprentice Service Opportunity Description and interviewing for an apprentice. Then the apprentice will fill in when necessary or take over the position for which she is apprenticing (see "Tools"). The shepherd coaches assist their team leaders in developing apprentices, and the team leaders do the same for their coordinators.

REMODELING: The administrative team may have resisted developing apprentices, which could be contributing to your reasons for remodeling. Set a date for each shepherd coach to write a Service Opportunity Description and recruit an apprentice ("Tools"). Encourage each shepherd coach to look at a team leader who has been serving effectively with her as a potential apprentice. If a team leader becomes an apprentice, she may wear "two hats" until she replaces herself as team leader. Be sure you're also recruiting an apprentice for yourself.

REFURBISHING: The more seasoned the administrative team, the more challenging it will be getting them to develop apprentices. They may feel they've been doing the job just fine on their own, which may be true, but that's not team building. Have each shepherd coach read this chapter and lead a discussion on the value—to themselves and to the ministry—of developing apprentices. Follow the guidelines in "Building" and "Remodeling."

Tools

Review chapter 14 for guidelines in writing a Service Opportunity Description. Following is a sample apprentice Service Opportunity Description for Anywhere Church.

ANYWHERE CHURCH WOMEN'S MINISTRY

Service Opportunity Description for: *Special Events Apprentice*
Your Shepherd: *Special Events Shepherd Coach*

PURPOSE: To support, assist, and learn all aspects of the special events shepherd coach position and prepare to assume the shepherd coach role when necessary.

Service Requirements:
• Willing and able to fill in for the special events shepherd coach as needed.
• Must love to have fun and enjoy hospitality.
• Event planning experience is helpful, but not required.
• Organized and flexible.
• Creative and willing to think beyond what seems possible.
• Access to computer and email.
• Willing to make this position your focused area of ministry service.

Service Responsibilities:
1. Help develop and lead the special events team.
2. Assist the special events shepherd coach with all aspects of special events.
3. Meet monthly with special events shepherd coach to pray, brainstorm, and connect.
4. Attend an event or meeting in the absence of the shepherd coach.
5. Assist with recruiting and training new team members.
6. Assist in developing Service Opportunity Descriptions.
7. Help with special projects as assigned.

Service Duration:
A shepherd coach apprentice is a long-term and committed role, so please consider carefully if you are willing to make this your primary area of service. You would assume the role of shepherd coach should she need to leave her position.

I agree to all of the above:_____

Those able to help others, those with gifts of administration.

— 1 CORINTHIANS 12:28

Team-Building Project

Invite shepherd coaches, team leaders, coordinators, and their apprentices to attend a "Two Are Better Than One" training session.

1. Read Ecclesiastes 4:9–12; Mark 6:7–13; 14:13; and Luke 10:1. Lead a group discussion on the value, purpose, and enjoyment of doing projects with another person.
2. Ask why someone might not want an apprentice. You may hear:
   - Fear that I won't be needed anymore.
   - An apprentice might do the job better than me.
   - It takes too long to explain how to do a task.
   - It's easier to do everything myself.
   - I don't know how to find and develop an apprentice.
3. Conduct this exercise:
   - Have the shepherd coaches, team leaders, and coordinators sit in chairs at a table.
   - Using ribbon or string, tie their hands behind their back.
   - In front of each woman, place a cup of water with a tight fitting lid that has a hole for a straw.
   - Next to the cup lay a straw still in the wrapper.
   - Instruct each woman to open the straw, place it through the lid, and take a drink of water (without untying her hands).
   - After they have struggled for a few minutes, let anyone who has an apprentice receive help from the apprentice.

This is a visual none will soon forget. Discuss the value of having someone to help you in challenging circumstances—or better yet help you avoid them altogether.

Leader to Leader

The value of an apprentice was one of the hardest concepts for me to instill in the administrative team. I actually did an exercise with the shepherd coaches that I only recommend you try if you have a group of women who are agile enough to sit on the floor. I tied each shepherd coach's hands together behind her back and had the coaches lie down flat on their back on the floor. Then I instructed them to try to get up—with the caveat that those with an apprentice could receive assistance from their apprentice.

I was nervous about doing this exercise, but one shepherd coach who was struggling on the floor without anyone to help her up said that experience was the only thing that resonated with her. She finally "got it," promptly started seeking an apprentice, and had one within a couple of months. I had been trying for over six years to get her to embrace the concept of an apprentice. She then took the "Two Are Better than One" training to her team leader meeting and her visual was the same exercise.

For the administrative team and their teams to appreciate the importance and value of an apprentice, you also must have one. I went through several apprentices over the years. If someone was willing to take on the ministry leadership, she wasn't always willing to take on the role of apprentice—to walk beside me and learn; sometimes she wanted to walk in front of me and lead. Others just wanted to spend more time with me. I realized that finding one person to replace me wasn't going to be easy: one person who shared my dream and vision for the ministry and was humble enough to receive mentoring in how to lead it. You may have that same problem, and so did Jesus.

We've discussed Jesus training His "inner core" of Peter, James, and John, whom He groomed to be key leaders in carrying on His ministry. Jesus primarily focused on Peter as His apprentice. Jesus said in Matthew 16:18 that He would build His church on Peter, the rock, and it appears that Peter was one of the key leaders in the early Christian church.

Like Jesus, look for your "inner core" of two or three team members who show potential to serve as your apprentice and as the future ministry visionary director. Spend extra time mentoring and including them in key decisions and meetings. Wait and see who emerges as your "rock." As I helped each shepherd coach develop ownership of her respective area, I prayed and watched. Eventually, one shepherd coach became my apprentice, and she had an apprentice ready and trained to take her place on her team.

Don't become discouraged if the shepherd coaches hesitate to seek apprentices. Keep encouraging them to do so. The future of the ministry depends upon it. If every level of leadership develops apprentices, the ministry can focus on its real purpose—serving your church.

Finishing Touches

- Having an administrative team in place is a huge accomplishment, but that team is fragile: It can change in a heartbeat. Someone suddenly has to move or becomes ill—any number of things can happen and, just as you're celebrating a full team, there's an empty chair. An apprentice helps you avoid the empty chair.
- You'll need to participate in the shepherd coach apprentice interviews because the apprentices they select might become members of the administrative team someday.
- In picking an apprentice, observe women who faithfully serve and show signs of wanting more responsibility.
- Someone may want to be an apprentice because she wants your attention or to spend time with you but has no intention of ever replacing you—that's not a true apprentice.

Mentoring Moment

Apprentices are essential to the longevity of a ministry.

CHAPTER 19

Jesus Met with His Team

When they were in the house again, the disciples asked Jesus about this. He answered.

—MARK 10:10–11

The Cornerstone

Many Scriptures refer to Jesus gathering His apostles together away from the crowds. Often they met in a home or a quiet place where Jesus could talk with his disciples privately (Mark 4:10–12; 7:17–23; 9:11–13, 26–31; 13:3–37). Mark 9:30–31 specifies that *"Jesus did not want anyone to know where they were, because he was teaching his disciples."* The disciples asked questions and He answered—explaining a miracle He had performed, illuminating the meaning of a parable He had told, or describing His future plans (Mark 8:31–32; 9:31a–32; 10:32–34). He invested time in meeting with His team.

The Blueprint

Establish a day of the week, time, and place to hold monthly team meetings. Consistency works well for planning; for example, the second Thursday each month, 7:00 P.M. to 9:30 P.M., in a church meeting room. Weeknights work best because weekends are difficult for people to attend regularly, and you may have team members who work during the day and can only attend at night. Meet with your team bimonthly for business meetings. On the opposite month, enjoy a fellowship Bible study meeting, discussed in the next chapter.

Customize

BUILDING: In the recruiting interview, inform prospective team members that they will be attending a monthly meeting and include this in the Service Opportunity Description.

REMODELING: If you haven't held regular team meetings, this is your chance as a ministry visionary director to cast a new vision and goal of monthly team meetings. When you make the announcement, have a date, time, and place for the first meeting, then discuss what will work best for everyone in the future.

REFURBISHING: If you haven't held regular team meetings, follow *Remodeling*. If you have held meetings, try redesigning them according to this chapter.

Tools

A well-planned and thought-out agenda prevents the need for calling "emergency meetings" or having frequent meetings. The agenda keeps your time together focused and productive, and everyone appreciates only having to make time for scheduled meetings. Following is a sample agenda for an administrative team business meeting.

Anywhere Church Women's Ministry

Shepherd Coach Monthly Meeting

Jesus . . . as the builder of a house has greater honor than the house itself.
For every house is built by someone, but God is the builder of everything.

— HEBREWS 3:3–4

- Opening prayer
- Devotion
- Exchange prayer cards (explained under "Team-Building Project")
- Pass out fasting prayers (also explained under "Team-Building Project")
- Review action items from last meeting's minutes
- Ministry visionary director report
- Shepherd Coach Area Reports
- Bible Study
- Woman to Woman Mentoring
- Support Groups
- Special Events
- Outreach
- Finance

- Upcoming Ministry Events Report by Shepherd Coach
- Bible Study
- Woman to Woman Mentoring
- Support Groups
- Special Events
- Outreach
- Finance

- Team-building project
- Announcements
- Next meeting: (Date, time, place)
- Close in prayer
- Refreshment and fellowship

Team-Building Project

Help shepherd coaches plan agendas for their meetings that communicate pertinent information from the administrative team meetings to their team leaders. They also need to incorporate time to hear reports on how each team leader's team is functioning. Then each team leader plans an agenda and meets with her coordinators. Shepherd coaches and team leaders might only need to meet with their teams quarterly or on an "as needed" basis.

1. To develop an agenda:
   - Write down things you and your team members want to cover.
   - Group similar items together.
   - Discard any topic that only involves one team member. Make a note to talk to her before or after the meeting.
   - At team meetings, discuss issues pertinent to all team members. Meet individually with team members to discuss issues pertinent solely to their team.
   - Invite each team member to give a concise report from her area of responsibility.
   - Discuss events occurring between meetings to prevent calling "emergency" meetings.
   - Keep the agenda to one page.
   - The agenda honors the meeting time. Announce in advance if it will run longer.

2. Guidelines for the business meetings:
   - Pray about the meeting.
   - Hand out the agenda at the beginning of the meeting.
   - Meet around a table so everyone sees each other and has plenty of room to take notes.
   - Have someone other than a team member take minutes on a laptop so team members can concentrate on the meeting. Offer this as a service opportunity for someone in the ministry.
   - Distribute the minutes to team members as a reminder of areas where

they need to take action. Start each meeting with a review of the last meeting's minutes.

~ Allow time after the meeting for a snack and fellowship.

~ Team meetings aren't "optional," but in an emergency, the apprentice could attend.

3. Prayer Cards and Fasting Prayers

On the agenda sample in "Tools," there were the following agenda points in the opening section of the meeting:

~ Exchange Prayer Cards—Each team member has a prayer card with her picture and her *personal* prayer requests. The team members exchange prayer cards at the monthly meetings, rotate prayer partners, and pray for each other's personal needs. Ask a member of your team to design simple prayer cards on the computer. The cards can be printed out on colorful card stock and placed in an envelope.

~ Pass Out Fasting Prayers—Many translations of Mark 9:29 suggest *"prayer and fasting"* as a vehicle to partner with God's power to accomplish His work. Like the disciples, your team might want to unite in praying and fasting for specific ministry needs. Every month, each team member submits a prayer request for her area of the ministry. These are ministry needs, not personal. The list is compiled and distributed at the monthly meetings. The team decides what day they want to fast and what they want to fast from. For example, our team fasted from sugar on Wednesdays and focused on praying for our fellow team members' ministry prayer requests. It's amazing how God honors the sacrifice and the unity.

Don't feel like you need to start these prayer ideas right away, but introduce them as a way to keep God at the head of your ministry and help the team prayerfully unite. Ask if they have other ideas.

Leader to Leader

One shepherd coach made this statement: "The secret to our success as a team is that we make our monthly team meetings a priority." Those words capture the heart of successful team meetings. It's a time of organizing and uniting as team members meet face to face and communicate in person with each other and with you. Don't let this precious time become a committee meeting or task force.

The team meets as a group to create synergy, but they also need the opportunity to meet with you individually. Ask team members not to present something new to you at team meetings or use the other team members' valuable time discussing something that only pertains to one person's team. Those are the types of issues to discuss with you one on one outside the team meeting. The team meetings should become times of action and encouragement without getting bogged down with endless discussion that could take place another time.

You don't want to be a committee of one, but you also don't want to lead a committee of many. If you structure the team the way I'm suggesting, you'll meet with the shepherd coach administrative team, and they'll each meet with their respective team leaders' teams, who meet with their coordinators' teams. You won't have to worry about who is picking up the speaker for the event or who is handling the food and decorations. That's the responsibility of the special events shepherd coach's team, and she'll give you a report at the administrative team meeting.

Scheduled, planned, productive meetings allow you to model the way the shepherd coaches should lead their team meetings. Come prepared, use the time wisely, and have a purpose and a plan. Team members will appreciate the meetings and take away the tools they need to lead their teams.

Inform potential team members that attendance at team meetings is essential. Apprentices can attend the meeting in a team member's place, but reserve this option for emergencies only. That might seem strict, but you can't build a unified team with substitutes—you need to meet with the group of people responsible for the ministry. This is the team who will function in your absence. You're about the Lord's work; you want to convey reverence and importance to your meetings for the work you do for Him.

Laurie Beth Jones in her book *Teach Your Team to Fish* quotes a corporate director who said, "When values are internalized, the need for rules diminishes."

When the team has internalized the value of the work accomplished at a team meeting, they would hold the team meeting even if you weren't there to lead it.

Finishing Touches

- It's worth repeating that topics at team meetings should involve *all* team members. This takes practice, but once the team and you experience the increase in productivity of your meetings when you only address matters that affect everyone, you'll see the wisdom.
- Answer team members' questions about why or how you did something but pick the appropriate time, which might not be at a team meeting. Jesus didn't always answer the disciples' questions in the moment, but He did take them aside and explain His actions.
- Address an individual team member's issues or questions with her personally.
- Don't take votes. A majority vote is never an ideal solution to those in the minority. Present issues so everyone feels like a winner. Much time is wasted in meetings discussing what color the tablecloths should be — everyone will have an opinion. Eliminating votes doesn't mean you're a dictator — certainly no one would characterize Jesus that way.

> *Jesus appropriately exercised the authority He had. His was clearly not a democratic organization. When He told His disciples to prepare a boat to cross the Sea of Galilee, He didn't first call for a committee meeting. When He decided to head for Jerusalem, He didn't call for a show of hands to see how many agreed. He exercised his authority, yet He also recognized the authority of His Father; 'Yet not what I will, but what you will.'*
>
> —Bob Pritchard and Ray Briner, *Leadership Lessons of Jesus*

Here's an example of arriving at an agreeable and good solution without taking a vote: We were looking for a place for our fall planning retreat. One option was a home in Palm Springs with a pool, but everyone would have to share beds; the other home was in the mountains and everyone would have her own bed, but no pool. It's doubtful a lengthy discussion of the details of the two places would end in a consensus, so I simply asked, "Would you rather have a pool or your own bed?" Unanimously: "Our own bed." Decision made —we went to the mountains.

Mentoring Moment

Developing a team that could carry on without you is going to take an investment of time and energy. It won't happen quickly, but it will happen if you patiently mentor and meet with the team.

Jesus Fellowshipped with His Team

While Jesus was having dinner at Levi's house, many tax collectors and "sinners" were eating with him and his disciples. — MARK 2:15

The Cornerstone

The Gospels often mention Jesus and the apostles eating, breaking bread, and fellowshipping together in someone's home (Mark 1:29–31; 3:20). Jesus' last time with His team was a meal in the upper room (Mark 14:12–31). When Jesus appeared to the disciples after the resurrection, He went to the home of the two men He met on the road and *"when he was at the table with them, he took bread, gave thanks, broke it and began to give it to them"* (Luke 24:30). The next morning, *"Jesus said to them, 'Come and have breakfast'"* (John 21:12).

The Blueprint

Last chapter, we talked about establishing regular team meetings; hopefully, you've been working on a scheduled day, time, and place each month to meet. Now, incorporate fellowshipping meetings into this schedule. Evaluate your annual ministry calendar to determine major events that include the whole team and schedule the administrative business meetings for the month prior to, and the month of, those events. On open months, plan a fellowship night.

Like the administrative business meetings, fellowship nights shouldn't be optional. Establish the atmosphere that this night is about building relationships with each other. As leaders, we are focused on getting the job done, but we also need time to just "hang out" together. Fellowship nights also are an opportunity to mature in the Lord together by doing a Bible study or discussing a book the team is reading.

Always include a meal with fellowship. It's not about the food, it's about the fellowship, so nothing elaborate. Jesus set the example throughout His ministry—He ate and fellowshipped with His team. They were family. There's something endearing about breaking bread together as you talk—even if it's business.

Customize

BUILDING: Look at your forecasted ministry calendar of events and plan team meetings and fellowship/Bible study nights. The ministry schedule might require two consecutive months of business meetings, or even three—that's OK. Just be sure you sprinkle in fellowship months.

REMODELING: Fellowship time might be just what the team needs to work on some of the issues leading to the remodel. Select one of the Bible studies in "Tools" or a book from chapter 16 "Tools," page 117, to help the team grow together or mend if needed.

REFURBISHING: The team may know each other well from working together, so introduce a fellowship and Bible study or book discussion night to mature in the Lord and socialize together. Select one of the Bible studies in "Tools" or a book from chapter 16 "Tools," page 117.

Tools

Suggested Bible studies to do together as a team:
Jesus on Leadership: Becoming a Servant Leader by C. Gene Wilkes
Face-to-Face with Mary and Martha: Sisters in Christ by Janet Thompson
Face-to-Face with Euodia and Syntyche: From Conflict to Community by Janet Thompson

Face-to-Face with Priscilla and Aquila: Balancing Life and Ministry by Janet Thompson
A Woman's Guide to Servant Leadership by Rhonda Kelley
Jesus By Heart by Roy Edgemon and Barry Sneed

Team-Building Project

1. Schedule times to fellowship individually with team members and discover what's happening in their lives outside the ministry.
2. Solicit ideas from the team for a quarterly fun day together, but find something they *all* enjoy. Suggestions: Have the team over to your house for a barbecue or to watch a "chick flick" and have everyone bring their favorite munchies. Go to a teahouse, miniature golfing, bowling, a women's conference, or the beach. Plan a potluck and invite each team member to bring her family or a guest. Or take up a collection, if the ministry doesn't have a budget, and order pizza or takeout food.
3. For fellowship/Bible study night, select a Bible study that focuses on being better leaders or enhancing relationships with each other and with the Lord. In chapter 22, we'll talk about having a "theme" for each year; the Bible study or book you choose should center on that theme. Have the shepherd coaches lead discussion to provide them an opportunity to sharpen their leadership skills.
4. If this seems a big stretch for you, read the Scriptures again from this chapter to remind yourself how Jesus ate and fellowshipped with His team. Pray that God gives you the same insight and wisdom in balancing work for the kingdom with fellowship for the soul.

Leader to Leader

The first few years leading the ministry, I was *all* business. The team met every month and stuck to the agenda. Then, I realized that Jesus ate with His apostles, and it wasn't always business. So, I initiated a fellowship/Bible study night. I chose leadership studies or a book for us to read. We alternated a business meeting one month, and a fellowship/Bible study meeting the next month. On Bible study night, we first ate dinner together, and then we did our study, which was led by one of the team members. We did potluck or took up a collection and ordered takeout.

Our December meeting was a Christmas celebration on our regular meeting night. We dressed up, went out to dinner, laughed over a white elephant gift exchange, and enjoyed good food and fun with each other.

If you're an "all business" kind of person, pray to see value in getting to know the team members personally. Spending relaxed, casual, but still meaningful time together is healthy and enhances team dynamics. The time still has purpose—developing relationships within the team.

Finishing Touches

⁓ You'll be tempted to spend extra fellowship time with team members you feel closest to or those who are in your "inner core." That can cause friction with other team members. The team's satisfaction and cooperation derives from how valued and appreciated *each woman* feels.

⁓ When Jesus went to Peter's mother-in-law's house, He found her sick. Jesus healed her and stayed for dinner (Matthew 8:14–15). Make time to have a cup of coffee or meal with your individual team members. Something in one woman's personal life might prompt it, or make it a point to find out what is happening in each woman's life. People need to know you care about them for more than just what they can accomplish.

Mentoring Moment

You'll experience a deeper level of camaraderie on the team as you learn about each other's lives over pizza, and then study God's Word together and how it applies to Christian leadership.

Jesus Confronted Difficult Situations

When evening came, Jesus arrived with the Twelve. While they were reclining at the table eating, he said, "I tell you the truth, one of you will betray me — one who is eating with me." They were saddened, and one by one they said to him, "Surely not I?" "It is one of the Twelve," he replied, "one who dips bread into the bowl with me."
— MARK 14:17–20

The Cornerstone

Jesus confronted Judas and told him He knew of the plot against Him. Jesus didn't mince words, avoid the topic, or tell others behind Judas' back. Later that night, Jesus confronted Peter twice, telling him that he would deny Him before the end of the night, despite Peter's protest that he would never do such a thing (Mark 14:27–31, 37–38).

One day, Jesus heard His disciples arguing as they walked along the road. When they arrived in Capernaum, He confronted them by asking, "'*What were you arguing about on the road?' But they kept quiet because on the way they had argued about who was the greatest. Sitting down, Jesus called the Twelve and said, 'If anyone wants to be first, he must be the very last, and the servant of all'*" (Mark 9:33–35).

When the situation called for it, Jesus was "*indignant*" (Mark 10:13-16) and "*rebuked*" (Mark 8:33; 16:14) His team members.

The Blueprint

When conflict inevitably rears its ugly head, address it immediately. As leaders, we must confront a disruptive team member, two team members feuding, or any form of conflict. Often, we mistakenly think that, as Christians, we must endure someone working against us, not doing her share, or undermining our leadership; but being a Christian doesn't mean ignoring problems or problem people. Jesus certainly didn't. It's best and biblical to deal directly with the situation and follow the guidelines in Matthew 18:15–17.

When Jesus heard His apostles arguing, He intervened and mediated by addressing the issue with all of them, and then used the resolution as a teaching experience. Infighting will destroy the unity of the team and compromise the work of the ministry (Philippians 4:2–3). As the ministry visionary director, you must deal directly with conflict on your own team of shepherd coaches, modeling and teaching them how to address conflict on their teams.

In the "Tools" section below, "7 Biblical Steps to Resolving Conflict" offers principles that apply to resolving all conflict, and the skits and case study in the appendix are visual applications of these steps. Agreeing to a "Team Conflict-Resolution Covenant" (also in the "Tools" section) helps minimize future conflict.

Customize

BUILDING: Give each team member a copy of "7 Biblical Steps to Resolving Conflict" from the "Tools" section below. They may have problems with the first step—going to the other person even when they think the other person is at fault. Stress that Matthew 18:15–17 tells us to do this before we serve or worship—in other words, before gossip starts and the work of the Lord becomes compromised. Ask each member to agree to a "Team Conflict-Resolution Covenant" (see "Tools"). When you've completed the team by filling all the shepherd coach positions, incorporate the skits and case study in the appendix into a team meeting, retreat, or miniretreat.

REMODELING: Team problems often result from not knowing the right way to resolve issues. Introduce current and new team members to "7 Biblical

Steps to Resolving Conflict" and the Team Conflict-Resolution Covenant (in "Tools"). Have team members act out the skits (found in the appendix) as a visual way of applying the steps.

REFURBISHING: The team may have found ways to resolve issues, but their team members could benefit from reading "7 Biblical Steps to Resolving Conflict" and the Team Conflict-Resolution Covenant . Go over both of these with team members and ask them to introduce the concepts to their teams. The skits and case study in the appendix are valuable tools for everyone in the ministry.

Tools

Leading Women Who Wound by Sue Edwards

Face-to-Face with Euodia and Syntyche: From Conflict to Community by Janet Thompson

The Peacemakers: A Biblical Guide to Resolving Personal Conflict by Ken Sande

7 Biblical Steps to Resolving Conflict
(From *Face-to-Face with Euodia and Syntyche: From Conflict to Community* — Janet Thompson)

Pray together before going through these steps.
1. *Take the initiative to resolve the conflict* (Matthew 5:23–24; 18:15–17). The moment you sense a problem in your relationship, take the first step toward righting it—even if you think the other person was wrong and you've done nothing to provoke her. If possible, approach her face-to-face. Letters, email, texting, or phone calls seldom resolve conflict because we can't read each other's face, eyes, or body language.

If face-to-face is not feasible, use the phone so you can proceed with the following steps. But the phone is *only* an option when it's the only option. If she won't meet with you alone, offer to bring a non-biased mediator; and if that's not agreeable, then meet together with a pastor from your church.

2. *Focus on goals bigger than your personal differences* (Ephesians 4:3 and Philippians 3:12-14). Before starting a discussion, establish that the relationship is more important than any disagreement.

3. *Listen attentively as the other person tells how she sees the situation* (Proverbs 18:13 and Proverbs 29:20). Let her speak first while you listen with your heart, eyes, and ears without becoming defensive or angry. Empathize as you hear the hurt in her voice. Don't interrupt. Let her complete her story.

4. *Validate the other person's feelings without minimizing her concerns* (James 1:19–20). Acknowledge her points, without arguing or challenging. Then ask if she'll listen to you.

5. *Tell your story* (Proverbs 18:17). Indicate you understand how she may have perceived the situation differently than you meant it. Avoid assigning blame. It's OK to let her know how the situation hurt your feelings.

6. *Apologize and ask forgiveness for your part in the disagreement* (Colossians 3:13; 1 John 1:9–10). Don't expect her to say she's sorry or to ask for forgiveness. Forgive with no hidden agenda or expectations.

7. *Discuss how to avoid future conflict* (Proverbs 17:14). Set ground rules for the relationship. Close with prayer.

When you're working through an issue with someone, place a copy of the "7 Biblical Steps to Resolving Conflict" in front of both of you. The biggest problem for the one calling the meeting will be to remain quiet and attentive while the other person tells her side of the story first. This takes practice.

TEAM CONFLICT-RESOLUTION COVENANT

~ We agree to use the "7 Biblical Steps to Resolving Conflict."

~ We agree not to make negative assumptions or question each other's motives. Instead of assuming that the other person had hurtful motives, we'll give the benefit of the doubt that she had good intentions.

~ We agree to keep the emotion in our conversations to a minimum and to speak calmly and kindly to each other, avoiding blaming statements.

~ We agree not to allow anger to fester and become resentment and bitterness. We will go directly to the person who offended us.

~ We agree that if a team member begins telling us about a problem with another team member, we'll stop the conversation before it continues and advise her to go to that person with the complaint.

Team-Building Project

1. Act out and discuss the skits in the appendix, which depict a practical application of the "7 Biblical Steps to Resolving Conflict." Feel free to change the circumstances to fit your group.

2. Discuss how you and the team rate yourselves in typically dealing with conflict. Answer the following questions with Always, Sometimes, Occasionally, or Never. When faced with conflict, how often do you:
   ~ Avoid it?
   ~ Ignore it?
   ~ Let someone else deal with it?
   ~ Tell others about the problem instead of telling the problem person?
   ~ Take it personally?
   ~ Remain objective?
   ~ Deal with it biblically, directly, and resolutely?

3. The following is a team and leadership grievance report from Anywhere Women's Ministry. Give a copy of this report to team members and discuss their responses with the goal of dealing with potential issues before they become problems. Also discuss how applying what you've learned from *The Team That Jesus Built* could resolve most of these problems.

Anywhere Church Women's Ministry Grievance Report
Check any issues that you've encountered in ministry.

A Team Member's Problems with Her Leader

THE TEAM LEADER:

__Interferes with a job I was asked to do.

__Does not know how to approach me and the others in leadership.

__Is going behind me and changing what I do.

__Is not allowing me to serve where I want.

__Is not bringing new women onto teams or into leadership.

__Is not giving me the opportunity to use my gifts.

__Gives unclear responsibilities. (OR is unclear when outlining responsibilities.)

__Does not communicate with me.

__Plays favorites.

__Does not express appreciation.

__Allows for leadership cliques.

A Leader's Problem with a Team Member

THE TEAM MEMBER:

__Consistently disagrees with me as a leader.

__Isn't committed to the team effort.

__Questions my leadership.

__Competes with other team members instead of building unity.

__Disagrees with and doesn't support the team's purpose and goals.

__Engages in power struggles.

__Avoids change/holds on to traditions, to the team's detriment.

__Has no follow-through; fails to complete agreed-upon tasks.

__Does not meet deadlines.

__Does not attend planning meetings.

__Consistently arrives late.

__Is not promoting or attending events.

__Only supports her own activities.

__Won't graciously step down from her position when asked.

Team Members' Problems with Each Other

A FELLOW TEAM MEMBER:

__Takes over others' responsibilities without notice.

__Redoes someone's job.

__Hurts others' feelings.

__Shows jealousy.

__Gossips.

__Engages in backbiting.

__Forms cliques.

__Is disloyal to teammates.

4. If you have an actual conflict issue on the team, ask if the disagreeing parties would be willing to go through the "7 Biblical Steps to Resolving Conflict" while the other team members observe. Or use the case study in the appendix, and let them practice using the steps.

Leader to Leader

Conflict can be subversive and undermining or overt and obvious. It may arise over a shepherd coach refusing to develop a team or recruit an apprentice because she's convinced she can do everything better, or not participating in team meetings or following through on responsibilities. A personal disagreement can erupt between two team members, or between a team member and the ministry visionary director. Conflict can result from an outright act of belligerent or disrespectful behavior or simply a clash of personalities or miscommunication. There are many possible conflict scenarios, but pride is always at the root of conflict.

> ∼ I think *my* way is better than yours, and *I* am going to prove it to you or to others.
> ∼ *I* don't like what you're doing so *I* am not going to cooperate.
> ∼ *I* didn't get my way and it makes *me* mad.
> ∼ *I* feel overlooked for all *my* efforts.
> ∼ *I* can do it better *myself*.
> ∼ *I'm* not happy on this team.

Do you see the pattern? It centers on me, myself, and I. As leaders, if we remember that God hates pride and a leader is a servant, we can quickly put out the conflict fire in our own hearts and help others do the same. Other times, we need to be told, or we need to tell someone, the ego fire is burning out of control.

In the best interest of the ministry, you may need to remove a problem person from the team — not from your life or church or even the ministry. In fact, just the opposite, because she probably needs extra attention in her spiritual walk and in understanding what it means to serve the Lord selflessly. Perhaps there's another place she can serve, but leaving her on the administrative team or in a leadership role will result in dissension and God's work being compromised.

I've had betraying Judases, Peters who left when the going got rough, and doubting Thomas team members — how about you? I don't like conflict — most of us don't — but it goes with the role of leader. In chapter 2, I discussed the difficulties I had with my first team and how God used that experience to grow me as a leader who follows Jesus' example. I couldn't run away, deny, or ignore conflict or problem people. Just like Jesus, I had to deal with the situation directly and biblically.

That's when I wrote "7 Biblical Steps to Resolving Conflict" and the "Team Conflict-Resolution Covenant" and gave them to each shepherd coach to use in working out disagreements among their fellow team members, on their own teams, and with me. The seven steps work because they're biblically based. I later wrote the Bible study *Face-to-Face with Euodia and Syntyche: From Conflict to Community*, which I recommend for your team to do together because it covers issues like forgiveness, reconciliation, confronting, and dealing with difficult people. Euodia and Syntyche were feuding women on Paul's ministry team and their conflict was disrupting the team's work of spreading the gospel (Philippians 4:2–3).

I wish I could tell you that knowing how to resolve conflict eliminates it, but that won't be the case this side of heaven. However, knowing some of the trigger points of conflict, and what the Bible tells us about loving our neighbor more than ourselves, goes a long way towards minimizing the damage done by unresolved issues.

Finishing Touches

~ Don't lose faith in your leadership or take it personally when someone differs with your leadership style. It goes with the territory. You're the point person—out in front—and you're going to encounter the blows of attack first. Satan doesn't want Christian leaders succeeding and raising up followers who lead in an ethical, moral way. Satan will use every means available—even people closest to you—to try to stop you and the team.

~ If you have a disloyal team member or someone causing a disturbance among the team, you must confront her and find a solution.

~ Even when you build the team following Jesus' principles, everyone won't get along. Jesus had to deal with conflict on His team, and we need to adjust and adapt to conflict on our teams. It hurts and can be discouraging, but don't submit to thinking: *I can't believe this is happening* or *how can they do this to me?* Curb thoughts of feeling like you're a terrible leader, or that life's too short to take this kind of abuse! You might be tempted to quit, especially if you're a volunteer lay leader. Don't do it. God wants the ministry to succeed more than you do, and you'll be a better leader for the experience.

~ Take ownership of any part you have in the issue.

~ Confront the issue and the person using the "7 Biblical Steps to Resolving Conflict."

~ Continue with the good work the Lord has entrusted to you.

~ If confronting difficult situations is uncomfortable, seek help in finding ways to objectively and biblically confront them. Some suggestions would be:

    Read Christian books on conflict resolution and dealing with difficult people and circumstances. Put into practice what you learn.

    Consult with your pastoral staff.

    Have an accountability partner to alert you when you're avoiding conflict or difficult situations.

Mentoring Moment

If everyone agrees with you all the time, you probably aren't a decisive and effective leader.

Jesus Retreated with His Team

Jesus withdrew with his disciples to the lake. — MARK 3:7

The Cornerstone

Mark 3:1–6 records Jesus' encounter with the Pharisees regarding the healing of a man on the Sabbath. In the next verse (3:7), Jesus retreats with His team. After a big ministry event of teaching, preaching, healing, or performing a miracle, Jesus often retreated with His team. Jesus also retreated with His team right before a major miracle (vv. 4:35–36).

In Mark 6:31–32, Jesus said to the disciples, *"'Come with me by yourselves to a quiet place and get some rest.' So they went away by themselves in a boat to a solitary place."* Two verses later, Jesus commenced teaching again and the disciples helped Jesus with the miracle of feeding the five thousand (vv. 34–44), after which Jesus had the disciples leave in a boat and He *"went up on a mountainside to pray"* (vv. 45–46). Then Jesus calmed a storm and walked on water (vv. 47–52)!

The Book of Mark records five separate places where Jesus took His team to a quiet retreat to recharge, refuel, refresh, and strengthen their relationships with each other and with Him.

The Blueprint

Jesus knew His work requires stamina, courage, energy, and time! We can't give what we don't have. Leaders often are doers who don't consider resting and reflecting a good use of time—maybe even a waste of time. Sometimes we're so busy planning the event that we forget to fill up and refuel spiritually. Schedule time before and after an event to

- rest;
- affirm;
- encourage;
- pray;
- evaluate.

Once every year, plan to retreat for a weekend with the team to set goals and plan the ministry calendar for the next year. Sometime in the middle of the year, hold a one-day miniretreat in the local area, and invite apprentices to join.

Customize

BUILDING: You may be thinking, *I'm just forming the team and now you want me to retreat with them? That sounds like a big job. There's so much work to do—how are we going to find time to get away?* Jesus had a lot of work to do too in a very short time, yet He still saw the value of getting away from the crowd and having some R&R time with His team. You may want to start with a one-day miniretreat held at church or someone's home, but don't discount the value of a weekend retreat.

REMODELING: A weekend retreat is the perfect place to regroup and rethink the restructuring and remodeling of the team in a relaxed and informal atmosphere. In chapter 3 when I described that our team was down to three shepherd coaches and me, we still took our annual retreat and started the rebuilding process.

REFURBISHING: Retreating together may not be a new concept for the team, but if it is, they'll be rejuvenated and refreshed. You may need to convince them to take a break if they've been used to all work and no rest.

Tools

Following is a sample weekend retreat agenda where the theme was Choosing the Better Part.

CHOOSING THE BETTER PART

There is need of only one thing. Mary has chosen the better part, which will not be taken away from her. — LUKE 10:42 (NRSV)

FRIDAY, OCTOBER 24 — *"There is need of only one thing."*

8:00–8:30	Arrive at Janet's house. Pack up (Jane), pray (Millie), and leave
8:30–10:30	Carpool to our destination (stopping to buy lunch)
10:30–12:00	Check in, rooms (Jane), unpack food (Lisa), settle in (All), pray over house (Betty)
12:00–1:30	Lunch on the patio — Two team testimonies
1:30–4:30	Free time — relax and rest
4:30–5:30	Dinner preparation and table set (KP Chart)
5:30–6:30	Dinner and getting to know each other better (Millie)
6:30–7:00	Cleanup (KP Chart) and free time
7:00–7:30	Musical worship (JoAnn, Betty)
7:30–9:30	One testimony and complete last lesson of Jesus on Leadership Bible study (Lisa)
9:30– ???	Slumber party fashion show — Fun and fellowship and snacks (Candi)

SATURDAY, OCTOBER 25—*"Mary has chosen the better part"*

7:00–8:00   Personal time and quiet time with the Lord—Any early walkers or swimmers?

7:30–8:00   Breakfast preparation (KP Chart)

8:00–8:45   Breakfast and more getting to know each other (Millie)

8:45–9:15   Cleanup (KP Chart), prepare for day

9:15–9:30   Musical WORSHIP (JoAnn, Betty)

9:30–10:00   Devotional (Cathy)

10:15–11:00   Choosing our team family tree (Janet)

Choosing to HAVE an APPRENTICE (Janet)

Which is the better choice for mind, body, soul? (Janet)

11:00–11:15   Break/Snacks

11:15–12:15   Introduce next year's Bible study, *Face-to-Face with Mary and Martha* and next year's book, *Having a Mary Heart in a Martha World* (Janet)

Discussion of last chapters of *On Being a Servant of God* (Candi)

12:15–12:30   Lunch preparation (KP Chart)

1:30–1:30   Lunch and "Let's learn even more about each other" (Millie)

1:30–1:45   Cleanup from lunch—(KP Chart)

1:45–2:00   Worship in song (Betty, JoAnn) and PRAYER (Millie)

2:00–3:30   Plan 2004 calendar—Prayer monitor (Betty)

3:30–5:00   Smoothie time and craft (Candi)

Prayer card pictures (Jane)

5:00–6:30   Free time and dinner preparation (KP Chart)

6:30–7:30   Dinner and sharing (Millie)

8:00–9:30   Purpose for prayer partners (Janet)

New prayer cards (Jane)

Prayer partner exchange for 2004 (Betty)

Three testimonies

9:30–???   More fun (Candi)

SUNDAY, OCTOBER 26—*"Which will not be taken away from her"*

7:30–8:30	Breakfast preparation (KP Chart) and preparation for the day
8:30–9:30	Breakfast and "Have we missed anything we need to know about you?" (Millie)
9:30–10:00	Cleanup (KP Chart), free time
10:00–10:30	Choosing to prepare our hearts with guided reflective prayer (Janet)
10:30–12:00	Worship service —"Choosing the Better Part"

Millie	Opening Prayer
Betty and JoAnn	Worshipping in song
Candi	Scripture reading
Janet	Message
Jane and Lisa	Praise, affirmation, communion
Cathy	Closing prayer

12:00–2:00	Leftovers Are the Best Part
	Two testimonies

Pack, straighten up, pray.
On our way to choosing the better part!

A sample agenda for a miniretreat is given on the next page. This miniretreat was held at a shepherd coach's home.

AGENDA

Two Are Better Than One

It's better to have a partner than go it alone. Share the work, share the wealth. And if one falls down, the other helps, but if there's no one to help, tough! . . . By yourself you're unprotected. With a friend you can face the worst. Can you round up a third? A three-stranded rope isn't easily snapped.

—ECCLESIASTES 4:9–10,12 (THE MESSAGE)

SATURDAY, JULY 9, 2005

8:00 A.M.–5:00 P.M.

Miniretreat for Administrative Shepherd Coaches and Apprentices

8:00–9:00 A.M.	Arrive, welcome, breakfast, and cleanup	
9:00–9:30	Worship with Gig	
9:30–10:00	Prayerful worship	Led by Maribeth
10:00–10:15	Break	
10:15–10:30	Two Are Better Than One Exercise	
10:30–Noon	Mentoring Newer Team Members Candi and Brandii Roles The Team That Jesus Built Chapter Organization Charts	
Noon–1:00	Lunch and fellowship	

1:00–2:30	Recruiting exercises On the Phone and Practice In Person and Practice Use of Opportunity to Serve Profiles Potlucks How to Handle Someone Leaving a Position	Priscilla Betty Janet
2:30–2:45	Break	
2:45–3:45	Two Are Better Than One Exercise Extending Trust and Responsibility Who Are You Praying for as an Apprentice? On Our Knees Praying for Her Now	
3:45–4:45	Purpose-driven Huddles Individual Christmas Party for Teams Budget	Jane
4:45–5:00	Wrap-up Exercise	

Team-Building Project

Practical tips for planning an administrative team retreat.

1. Have the retreat in the fall so you can review the past year and plan the next calendar year. The first year, find a date that works for everyone, but future retreats are planned at the retreat. Like all other ministry dates, the retreat is on everyone's calendar.

2. Pray for the Lord to give you the purpose, theme, and Scripture for each retreat and the upcoming year. Use the theme to pick a Bible study and/or book to study together and pass them out at the retreat. Some of my retreat themes have been:

The Team That Jesus Built   —HEBREWS 3:3–4

Leading Out of Our Relationship with Christ

—HEBREWS 10:19A,22,24 (NLT)

Becoming a Servant Leader — MATTHEW 20:28 (TLB)

Keeping Your Heart for Ministry — JEREMIAH 3:15

Choosing the Better Part — LUKE 10:42 (NRSV)

3. Establish an agenda for the weekend (see the sample in "Tools" above).

4. Use mealtimes as an opportunity to get to know each other by having a grab bag of questions to pick from and answer at each meal.

5. Don't plan the retreat alone. Let the shepherd coaches know the theme and give each one an assignment. Delegate —
- Finding a location and securing accommodations — key things to look for are:
  - A table with sufficient chairs to accommodate everyone for meals and work time.
  - Sleeping arrangements.
  - Not too far away, but far enough so no one's tempted to go home.
- Food and meals:
  - Each person buys the food for and prepares one meal.
  - Each person brings what they like to drink and snacks to share.
- KP chart
- Carpooling
- List of what to bring
- Mealtime questions
- Calendar planning
  - Everyone brings her personal calendar and the team plans the upcoming year's events and meetings and puts the dates on their calendars.
- Fun activity
- Parts of the agenda
- Music for worship time

6. If you have a church budget, request funds for the retreat. If you don't,

estimate the cost of a retreat, divide by 12 months, and collect that amount from the team at the monthly meetings. Also solicit donations. Several years someone donated a mountain cabin for our retreat or the funds for us to rent one—what a blessing.

7. Leave room for flexibility and spontaneity.

Leader to Leader

Every fall, our administrative team went on a weekend planning retreat. We found a large cabin or home in the mountains or at the beach and settled in for a time of fun, calendar planning, vision casting, lessons, girl time, and relaxation. When we left this retreat, we had evaluated the current year and planned all our events for the next year.

Just like the monthly team meetings, these retreats aren't optional. The retreat dates are planned for the next year during the calendar planning time of each retreat, and when a new shepherd coach joins the team, she's given the calendar and advised to plan for the retreat. You can't bond without the whole team present. Just like with the monthly team meetings, you build value and commitment into the retreats.

As you read in the preface, I prayed for the Lord to give me a theme and planned the retreat agenda around the theme He revealed. Every year He gave me one, and He'll give you one as well. A major purpose of the weekend retreat is to plan the ministry calendar for the next year. The team is involved in this process and therefore is committed to the dates. You come home from the retreat with the next year already planned—that's a huge stress reliever.

Another outcome of the retreat is the strengthening of relationships. You get to know each other well when you live together for several days sharing the tasks of cooking, cleaning up, sharing rooms, and "hanging out" with no outside distractions. Retreating together may seem intimidating at first, but once you and the team share the experience, you'll appreciate the value Jesus saw in retreating with His team.

Finishing Touches

∽ Plan a local midyear Saturday miniretreat for the administrative team and their apprentices. Again, pray for a purpose and theme. Delegate duties. This retreat is a hands-on, how-to training day. Work on things like role-playing conflict resolution, recruiting help, and interviewing. The skits in the appendix are from one of our miniretreats.

∽ If you can't get away for an entire weekend, start with a miniretreat.

Mentoring Moment

God gave us rest, as well as food and drink, to fuel our bodies and our souls.

Jesus Empowered His Team

He appointed twelve—designating them apostles—that they might be with him and that he might send them out to preach and to have authority to drive out demons.
— MARK 3:14–15

The Cornerstone

When Jesus *appointed* and *designated* the disciples to be apostles, He also empowered them with the authority to carry out the jobs of preaching and driving out demons. Jesus gave the disciples, now apostles, assignments to do the work He had been doing and sent out His team to minister without Him! He married responsibility with the important binding thread of authority. Sometimes the team did well. Other times they failed miserably, but Jesus used their failures as teaching opportunities and then sent them out again. Jesus didn't jump in and do the task Himself, but continuously reminded His team that He had passed onto them the responsibility *and* authority, and His role was to confirm (Mark 16:20), defend (Mark 2:23–28; 7:5–13), and be their cheerleader and encourager!

The Blueprint

A ministry visionary director progressively and systematically gives away the ministry by delegating with empowerment. She teaches and trains the administrative team of shepherd coaches until they're ready to function on their own—equipped, empowered, enthusiastic, and entirely responsible for outcomes. Without this vision and goal, the ministry's success rises and falls with the ministry visionary director, and no one should put herself in that role. Jesus didn't; neither should we.

Synonyms for the word *empowerment* are: authorize, sanction, allow, and give power to. Developing a responsible team capable of functioning in your absence is a continuous process of

- delegating responsibility;
- granting authority;
- letting go;
- stepping aside.

Many leaders readily delegate a task and give assignments but don't grant the accompanying responsibility and authority. Admittedly, this is difficult because often, like the apostles, the team will disappoint you, which we talked about in chapter 17. However if you take back the task, you miss the opportunity for a positive teaching experience, and the team will never learn to do things themselves. *"A student is not above his teacher, but everyone who is fully trained will be like his teacher"* (Luke 6:40).

Customize

BUILDING: As you establish an administrative team, the long-range vision is to
- grant responsibility over their respective areas;
- equip them with knowledge, experience, role modeling, and mentoring;
- pass on the day-to-day operation of the ministry.

If you're just getting the team up and running, you may think it's too soon to empower them—it's never too soon. Otherwise, the ministry becomes yours with them trying to live out your vision. The team members will become dependent on you for approval and direction and may not feel they can function on their own. They won't share ownership of the ministry, so they won't feel bad reneging on responsibilities because they know you'll take over for them.

It's natural for the team to rely on you in the beginning when they're new and learning their roles. But if you've selected a team of women with gifts and talents in their areas of responsibility, you need to let them express their gifts without always looking over their shoulders or stepping in to do their jobs.

They'll have to earn this trust. You'll watch them in action and some will be empowered easier and sooner than others—these are your "inner core"—but the goal always remains for the entire team to function without you. Then these empowered shepherd coaches empower their own teams.

REMODELING: Perhaps relinquishing responsibility and authority has been difficult for you and that's why the team isn't taking their roles seriously or they're letting you do all the work. When a team member receives and accepts her significance to the ministry, she doesn't usually let you down. Empower and equip your remaining team members. It may take a while for them to feel confident that you really trust them, so you'll need to confirm and affirm often. As you add new team members, begin empowering them right away.

REFURBISHING: The team may be running like a well-oiled machine because you've delegated and empowered them. Or you may have a situation in which everyone is happy letting you, or a few, do most of the work. Evaluate your role as ministry visionary director and see if there are things you're still doing that someone else could readily do. If so, begin the process of passing on those tasks to the appropriate shepherd coaches, empowering each one with your trust.

Tools

In the *Woman to Woman Mentoring Training Leader's Guide,* I discuss the equipping and empowering of a training shepherd coach to train the mentors and mentees, a job I had been doing. As the ministry grew, I knew it was time to pass the baton in this area, and eventually other areas, following the same procedure. Here are empowerment steps to equip a shepherd coach to take over a role. This example is empowering a training shepherd coach, but you can customize the steps to whatever position you need to relinquish to a capable team member.

Empowerment Steps:

1. Observe you performing the role, just as Jesus had the apostles watch Him.
I had the person I interviewed and selected for the training shepherd coach watch me do an entire training several times.

2. Divide the job or responsibility between the two of you.
Gradually, I gave her portions of the training to teach with me.

3. Critique and evaluate her performance and the results.
We met after each of the training sessions to discuss the experience and answer her questions.

4. Progressively assign more of the role to her until she's performing on her own with you observing, evaluating, suggesting, and encouraging.
When she was ready to do the entire training on her own, I observed her in action and met with her after the training to discuss areas where she needed improvement, and commended and affirmed areas where she was excelling.

5. Release the role and let her do it on her own without you present.
After observing her in several trainings, I turned the entire training role over to her.

6. Occasionally check back to see how she's functioning in the role.
Periodically, I spot checked her performance by arriving at different times in the training.

7. If there's need for additional training, start the process over again—always with the goal of passing it on completely. If she's the right person for this position, she'll eventually "get it." If not, assign her to a different role and recruit another person to equip and empower. If things are going fine —let go.

When I saw she was doing an excellent job, I let go. The role of training shepherd coach belonged to her completely.

Team-Building Project

Team members feel empowered by the same things that empower you. Do you feel empowered in your role? I hope you can respond yes, because that's the feeling you want team members to experience. If your answer is no, what would make you feel empowered and how could you communicate that to those you report to in your church?

To evaluate the team's level of empowerment

1. Review with each shepherd coach her individual Service Opportunity Description. Evaluate together whether she has fully assumed the role, or are you still covering some of her responsibilities?

2. If she's assuming all her roles, encourage her to continue developing and empowering her own team.

3. If there are still roles she hasn't fully assumed, go through the empowerment steps (see the "Tools" section above) with the goal of her becoming fully responsible for the position.

4. When all team members are performing their roles, step back and let The Team That Jesus Built lead their teams and the ministry.

Leader to Leader

I've been fortunate to observe the leadership skills of Pastor Rick Warren since I joined Saddleback Church in 1987. In those early years, Pastor Rick was the stabilizing pillar of the church, and everyone wanted Pastor Rick to officiate at weddings and funerals, preach each Sunday, and attend the numerous functions at the church.

Pastor Rick realized that Saddleback couldn't center on him—or any one person—so he equipped, delegated, and empowered others to replace him in the daily functioning of the church. Because Pastor Rick systematically "gave away" daily tasks, Saddleback has grown into one of the largest megachurches in the world with numerous satellite churches.

Pastor Rick also subscribes to equipping and empowering church members to lead the various growing ministries in the church. I was one of those lay ministers allowed to follow a vision of a mentoring ministry. Pastor Rick understood that he couldn't do everything himself because the church would be limited to and bound by his energy and time. Saddleback has a team of pastors and members who caught Pastor Rick's vision, and he empowered them to carry out that vision—in his presence and in his absence. That also was my vision for the mentoring ministry, and one I eventually achieved.

When I was diagnosed with breast cancer, I didn't worry about the fate of the ministry. The administrative team was ready to take over. Each shepherd coach continued doing what she had been equipped and empowered to do, and the ministry went on without me. After recuperating, I assumed a limited role, but still lead the administrative team meetings.

When I took a sabbatical from the ministry for six months to write a book, our publicity shepherd coach pointed out that I couldn't remove myself from the day-to-day operation of the ministry as long as I was leading the meetings. I called her my Jethro (after Moses' father-in-law, who, as we learned in chapter 12, reminded Moses that he too must let go and delegate daily tasks for the greater good of the ministry, see Exodus 18:13–26). So my "Jethro" began grooming to be my apprentice by taking over the leadership of the meetings and developing an apprentice to one day replace her as publicity shepherd coach.

When my writing sabbatical was over, I knew the team no longer needed me at the helm. I couldn't and wouldn't return and take back what I had empowered my apprentice and the team members to do. They had replaced me in every area and the ministry was running beautifully. It was time for me to empower my apprentice to be the ministry visionary director and me to take on an advisory role.

I learned a great deal from watching Pastor Rick, and we both learned from the best leader who ever lived—Jesus. My vision for this book is to pass on some of that wisdom to you.

Finishing Touches

~ The team members won't always appreciate or understand why something is done a particular way until they start performing the task themselves.

~ Often, as team members take over particular roles, they'll want to add a different spin—maybe even tweak things significantly. Sometimes their way is better; other times they humbly tell you they now see the wisdom of your way. Your role is to remain humble either way.

~ It takes time to empower team members. Initially you might need to step in often, but you should be able to gradually back off and only intervene with constructive advice or when asked.

~ When Pastor Rick empowered his team, he was able to write life-changing books and start global missions projects. When I empowered the administrative team, I, too, was able to write life-changing books and take Woman to Woman Mentoring globally. What might God want you to do when you empower the team?

~ When shepherd coaches empower their teams and team leaders empower their teams and coordinators empower their teams, you have *The Team That Jesus Built.*

Mentoring Moment

A leader who has to have her hand in everything will cut off helping hands. There's no growth or new vision when a leader is task-oriented instead of empowerment-oriented.

CHAPTER 24

Jesus Served His Team

Now that I, your Lord and Teacher, have washed your feet, you also should wash one another's feet. I have set you an example that you should do as I have done for you. I tell you the truth, no servant is greater than his master, nor is a messenger greater than the one who sent him. —JOHN 13:14–16

The Cornerstone

John 13:1–17 is the famous passage where Jesus washes the feet of His team—even Judas who would soon betray Him. Jesus spent His entire ministry time on earth teaching, training, and equipping His team. Now it was time to set an example of the type of leaders He wanted them to become by humbly serving them. In doing this great and memorable act of service, He set an example of servant leadership for His apostles and for us to emulate.

The Blueprint

Effective leadership at any level is servant leadership. Serve the team members and they will follow you anywhere. What does it look like to be a servant leader?

～ Care about what team members care about.
～ Be their cheerleader.
～ Pray for them and let them know you're praying.

∾ Encourage them when they're down.

∾ Let them know they mean more to you than just the job they're doing.

∾ Be humble.

∾ Ask often, "How can I help you?"

Customize

BUILDING: The administrative team is going to need your help as they learn their responsibilities and build their own teams. You'll experience the reward for your time, energy, and emotional investment when you see how the ministry changes lives, starting with the women on the team.

REMODELING: Leaders usually serve others in the manner they feel served. Everyone on the team has a different way of feeling served by you. Look for ways to serve that match each team member's personality and area of service. Start with a footwashing service (see "Tools" and "Team-Building Project").

REFURBISHING: Serving the team doesn't mean doing everything for them or taking over all their responsibilities. That would be a disservice because the shepherd coaches won't learn to be servant leaders. The team probably is mature enough to experience and appreciate a footwashing service together (see "Tools" and "Team-Building Project"). Consider doing one at a Bible study/fellowship night or at a retreat or miniretreat.

Tools

Michael W. Smith's *The Second Chance* CD opens with a footwashing instrumental which is lovely to play during your footwashing ceremony. The CD also has songs to sing before and after, like: "Awesome God," "Above All," "Open the Eyes of My Heart Lord," and "Draw Me Close." To listen to the track go to http://new.music.yahoo.com/michael-w-smith/tracks/footwashing-instrumental—27202442.

Team-Building Project

Consider doing a footwashing ceremony with the team. Read John 13:1–17 together and begin the footwashing as team members commit to love each other as Christ loves them, with:

- Selfless love
- Serving love
- Unconditional love
- Responsible love

Footwashing Service of Commitment to Each Other

- Set up one chair, a foot basin, perfume, towels, and foot cream.
- Follow this rotation, which you'll modify for the number of shepherd coaches on the team.
- While washing, drying, or putting on lotion, each footwashing servant verbally commits to the person being served: "I will love you with *selfless* love, *serving* love, *unconditional* love, *responsible* love."

1. The shepherd coach being served sits in the chair and the remaining team members gather around.
2. First shepherd coach fills the foot basin with fresh, perfumed warm water, brings it to the chair, and places it before the seated coach's feet.
3. Seated coach puts her feet in the water.
4. Second coach washes the right foot.
5. Third coach washes the left foot.
6. Fourth coach dries the right foot.
7. Fifth coach dries the left foot.
8. Sixth coach puts cream on the right foot.
9. Ministry visionary director puts cream on the left foot.

- Shepherd coaches and ministry visionary director continue rotating into the position ahead of them. For example, first coach moves into the chair, and second coach empties and fills the tub with water. Everyone moves up one spot following the person in front of her until all have had their feet washed and committed to show each other: *selfless* love, *serving* love, *unconditional* love, *responsible* love.

Leader to Leader

Servant leadership is an area requiring diligent focus. Our tendency is to serve others in a manner we feel served. I love to learn, so I showered the team with books and researched new ways to help them grow as godly leaders. If one of my team members feels more served by time or fellowship than with tools for spiritual growth, I missed the mark. So ask yourself: How do I feel served, and how am I serving the team?

At one of our retreats, I asked to be put on the cleanup team for every meal so I could spend time with whoever was assigned to KP duty, and also so that person wouldn't have to do the cleanup alone. I chuckled that she always seemed more puzzled than served.

On our Bible study fellowship night, I served the team by helping make dinner so those with full-time jobs could just come and enjoy. I earnestly prayed for the team members and their families, and never asked anyone to do something I haven't or wouldn't do myself. I still have a long way to go in truly feeling I am a servant leader—the only way to lead like Christ.

Finishing Touches

- The footwashing ceremony at our team retreat was a powerful and tearful experience. For those committed to the service of the ministry, I believe it cemented a conviction to their role and to each other. However, I also had one shepherd coach call the next month and resign. She was one of the shepherd coaches with an unbelieving husband. It was too much of a commitment for her to make. The cost was too high.
- Footwashing isn't the only way to serve. Jesus served His disciples at the Passover supper (Mark 14:22–26). Consider serving communion (if appropriate in your church) at your annual and miniretreats or on a fellowship/Bible study night.
- Pray for discernment to know the type of service the team needs to receive from you and courage to act on what God reveals.

Mentoring Moment

"The measure of a leader is not the number of people who serve the leader, but the number of people served by the leader."

—Adapted from a quote by John C. Maxwell

CHAPTER 25

Jesus Granted Authority, Commissioned, and Released His Team

Jesus came to them and said, "All authority in heaven and on earth has been given to me. Therefore go and make disciples of all nations, baptizing them in the name of the Father and of the Son and of the Holy Spirit, and teaching them to obey everything I have commanded you. And surely I am with you always, to the very end of the age." —MATTHEW 28:18–20

When he had led them out to the vicinity of Bethany, he lifted up his hands and blessed them. While he was blessing them, he left them and was taken up into heaven. —LUKE 24:50–51

After the Lord Jesus had spoken to them, he was taken up into heaven and he sat at the right hand of God. Then the disciples went out and preached everywhere, and the Lord worked with them and confirmed his word by the signs that accompanied it. —MARK 16:19–20

The Cornerstone

Jesus issued the Great Commission to the 11 apostles during the time between His resurrection and ascension into heaven. Jesus passed on His authority to His team telling them: Everything you've seen me do, you too can do on your own. Not only can you do it, I command you to go out into the world and do it (Mark 16:15). The disciples accepted their new role and were successful!

The Blueprint

The Commissioning Process
- Empower.
- Grant authority.
- Commission.
- Bless.
- Release.
- Step back and let go.
- Support in prayer and in spirit.

As The Team That Jesus Built grows, you'll be less and less involved in the details of the everyday operations because the ministry will have outgrown what one person can oversee. Isn't that great news? If you hold on too tightly, the ministry can only be as big as your two hands. But when you equip, train, grant authority, commission, bless, and release the team, there are no limits to what the ministry can accomplish.

Customize

BUILDING: As you build the team, keep this chapter in mind—it's your ultimate long-range vision and goal. Develop an apprentice and your "inner core," and work on commissioning them first.

REMODELING: You may have lost some team members because they were ready for commissioning but you weren't ready to grant authority. Include your remaining team members in the restructuring process. Commission your apprentice and inner core and grant them authority, so you can focus on rebuilding the team with their help.

REFURBISHING: You're probably ready to have a commissioning ceremony to grant your refurbished team the authority to officiate the ministry in your absence while you expand the scope of the ministry or as you spend time fine tuning aspects you've "never had time to work on before." If you don't take an actual step of letting them know you're releasing them, they may be confused and think you're leaving them stranded.

Chapter 23

Tools

Commissioning Ceremony

- Invite family members, pastors, and the entire ministry to attend the commissioning ceremony.
- Open in prayer.
- Worship together with singing.
- Say something personal about each person you're commissioning and the role she has had in the ministry. Explain any new roles she'll be assuming. Express confidence and gratitude.
- Officially commission and grant each one the authority to lead their teams and make decisions for the ministry in your absence.
- Emphasize your availability for support, encouragement, and counsel.
- Explain any new role you might be assuming and how the change affects the ministry.
- Anoint each woman's head with perfumed oil and pray a blessing over her.
- Invite each woman to speak if she chooses.
- Answer questions from the audience.
- Close in prayer and song.
- Enjoy a time of fellowship and food.

Team-Building Project

1. When team members are ready for commissioning, orchestrate a commissioning ceremony (see "Tools").
2. Study the biblical history of anointing with oil. In the Old Testament, anointing with oil accompanied the commissioning of kings (1 Samuel 10:1; 16:10–13; 1 Kings 1:39). Team members aren't becoming queens, but they'll be assuming authority and responsibility.
3. You may take commissioning in steps: first with your apprentice and "inner core," then with other team members later. Your apprentice will be the new ministry visionary director. If you're continuing in the ministry or on staff, you could remain the official visionary who is accountable to the church and acting as a consultant to the team, while perhaps assuming new staff responsibilities or developing new areas of the ministry.

4. If you're staying on in the ministry, explain your role as visionary and ask for prayer as you work to further enhance and grow the ministry, maybe even beyond your church. Now you'll have time for that cup of coffee or lunch with each team member to pray for her and be her cheerleader.

Leader to Leader

If you've been following the steps in this book, you should be on your way to *The Team That Jesus Built* while God uses you to expand the ministry or act as a consultant to the shepherd coaches as they develop their own Teams That Jesus Built.

Jesus' team was prepared for His departure. Is yours? If the Lord took you home today to be with Him or moved you out of the area, are team members ready to step in and carry on without you? The time to prepare for this is now, not in the urgency of some crisis. Are you willing to pass on to the next generation of leaders all that God has entrusted to you? Are you teaching them to do the same? It's the only way that works. It's your legacy — *The Team That Jesus Built.*

Finishing Touches

As a child matures into an adult and leaves home, the parents have mixed emotions — proud of their child for developing into a capable man or woman, yet sad that the child is no longer dependent on them. Even sadder, however, are children who grow into adults but can't function on their own. The role of parents and leaders is to help children and teams become progressively independent of us and completely dependent on God.

You can do this, and I commend you for taking the difficult steps of equipping and commissioning a team prepared to carry on without you. It's the ultimate act of service and humility.

Mentoring Moment

Don't restrict the ministry to your limitations. Let it grow and let it go!

Epilogue

FIVE CHALLENGES FOR MINISTRY LEADERS

And the things you have heard me say in the presence of many witnesses entrust to reliable people who will also be qualified to teach others.

—2 TIMOTHY 2:2

To effectively pour your life into others throughout your lifetime . . .

1. YOU must take responsibility to continue developing in accordance with God's processing *all of your life!*
   When Christ calls you to Christian ministry, He intends to develop you to your fullest potential. Only you can stop Him.
2. YOU must continually be aware of God's processing of the younger leaders He puts in your life, and work with that process.
3. YOU must become the mentor and pass on what God teaches you.
   Be active in the selection of rising leaders. Pass on the torch. Teach what someone has taught you so you can train the next generation.
4. YOU must develop a ministry philosophy that honors biblical leadership values, embraces the challenges of our times, and fits your unique gifts and personal development if you expect to be productive over your whole lifetime.

5. YOU must believe and live your life under the conviction that mentoring others is not an option in the Christian life. It's a way of life ordained and instructed by the Lord in the Bible, and it's His plan for the growth and survival of the Christian faith.

"If you want to leave a legacy, you must look to people to carry it for you."
—JOHN C. MAXWELL, *The Maxwell Leadership Bible*

Appendix

MINISTRY ORGANIZATION CHART

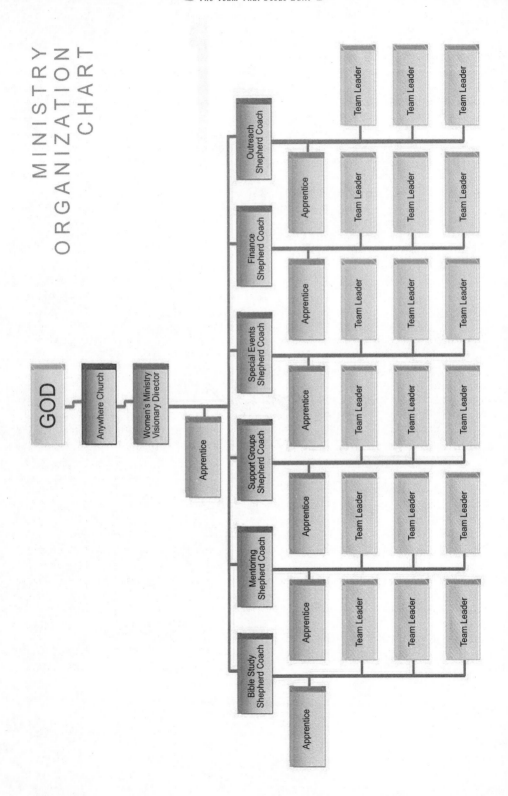

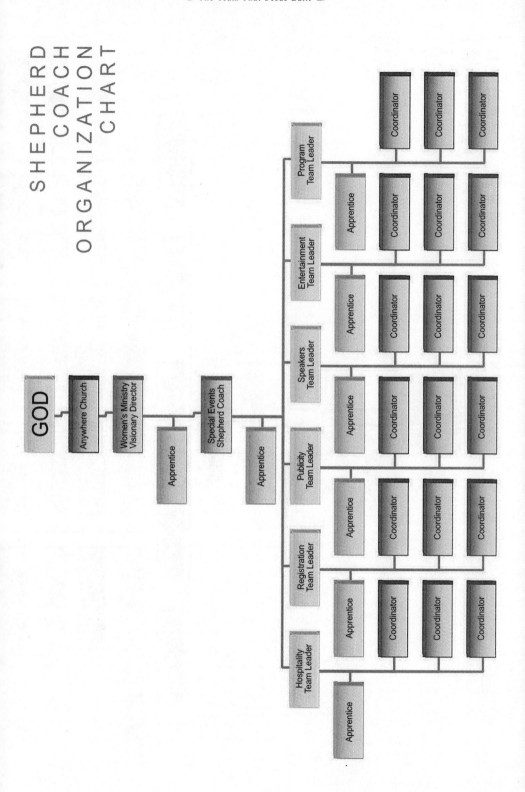

SHEPHERD COACH ORGANIZATION CHART

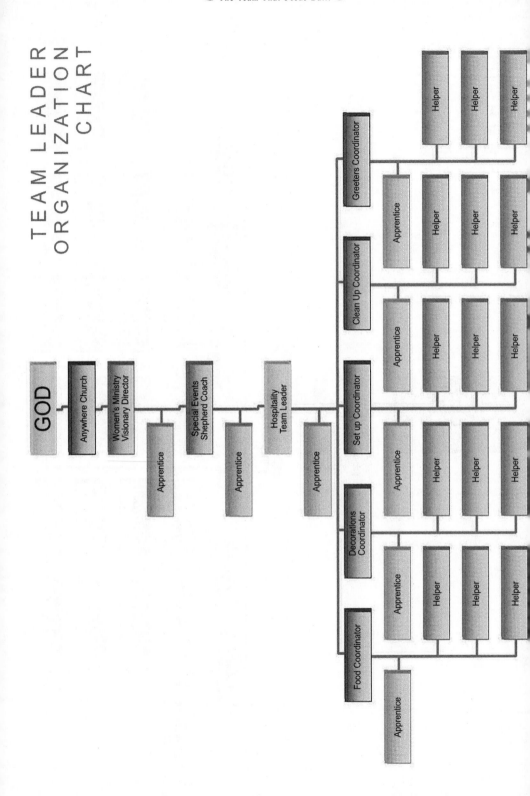

TEAM LEADER ORGANIZATION CHART

GOD

Anywhere Church

Women's Ministry Visionary Director

Apprentice

Special Events Shepherd Coach

Apprentice

Hospitality Team Leader

Apprentice

Food Coordinator
- Apprentice
- Apprentice
- Helper
- Helper
- Helper

Decorations Coordinator
- Apprentice
- Helper
- Helper
- Helper

Set up Coordinator
- Apprentice
- Helper
- Helper
- Helper

Clean Up Coordinator
- Apprentice
- Helper
- Helper
- Helper

Greeters Coordinator
- Apprentice
- Helper
- Helper
- Helper

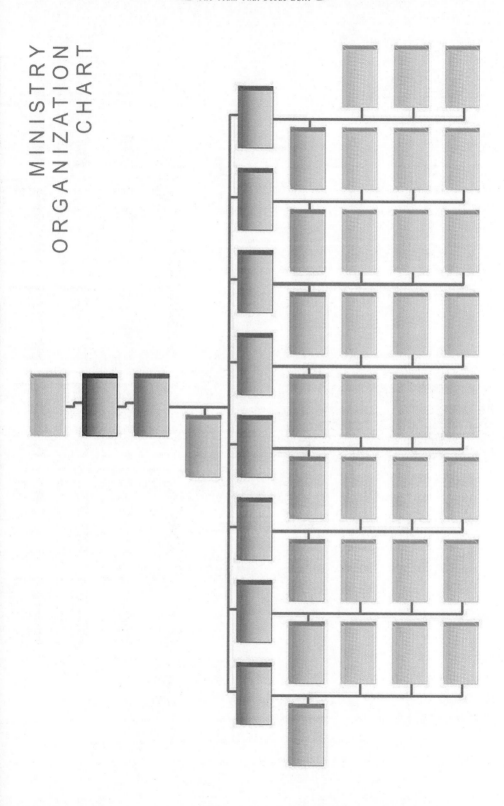

MINISTRY
ORGANIZATION
CHART

SHEPHERD COACH ORGANIZATION CHART

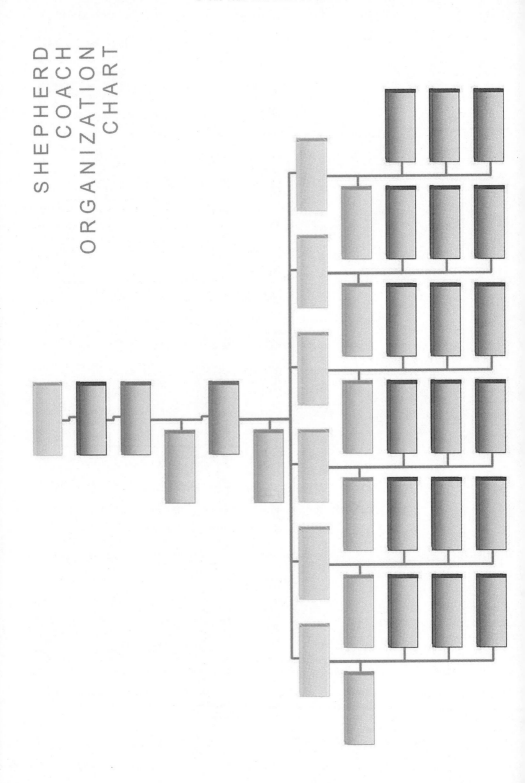

TEAM LEADER
ORGANIZATION
CHART

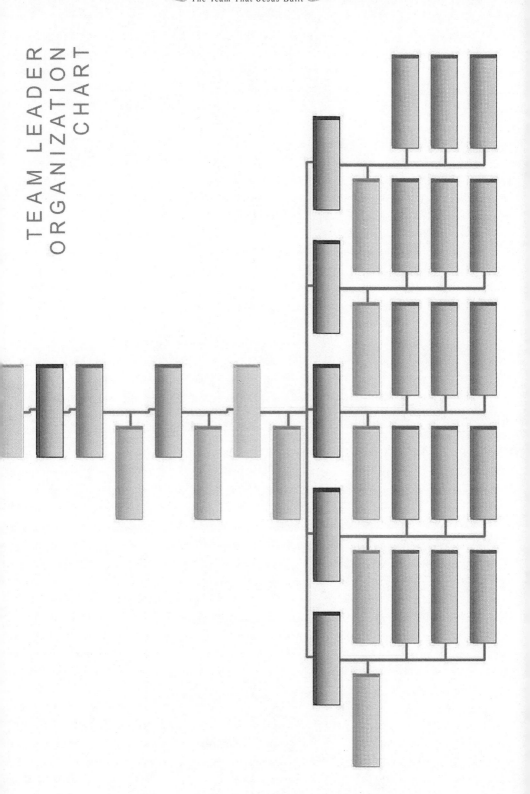

Conflict Resolution Skits

SKIT 1

WHAT'S A SHEPHERD COACH TO DO?

Setting the Stage:

- For brevity in the prompts, shepherd coach is "Coach" and visionary director is "Visionary."
  Coach 1 calls the visionary director and complains that Coach 2 said derogatory things behind Coach 1's back.
- Ask the group members what they would do if they were the visionary director.
- Lead a discussion of their answers, not indicating whether they're correct. Then have two people perform the following skit.

Coach 1 (*calling on phone.*)

Visionary: Hello?

Coach 1 (*agitated*): Hi. I need to talk to you. I just had to tell someone. Coach 2 said some hurtful things about me behind my back to the other team members.

Visionary: Have you talked to Coach 2 about this?

Coach 1: No, of course not! I have no desire to talk to her. That's why I'm calling you.

Visionary: Do you remember the Team Conflict-Resolution Covenant and how we committed to going through the *7 Biblical Steps to Resolving Conflict* with each other?

Coach 1 (*quietly*): Sort of . . .

Visionary: Do you know what the Bible says we should do when we're upset with someone?

Coach 1: No. What?

Visionary: Go get your Bible and let me show you.

Coach 1: OK, I have it. Now what?

Visionary: Turn to Matthew 18:15–17 and read to me what it says to do.

Coach 1 (*Reads out loud Matthew 18:15–17 slowly . . . like she is getting it.*)

Visionary: What's the first thing Jesus tells us to do—especially with a fellow Christian?

Coach 1 (hesitantly): Go to her and tell her my complaint. I guess that was the first of the seven steps, wasn't it?

Visionary: Yes, and can you see that doing anything other than that is gossip?

Coach 1: No. What do you mean?

Visionary: Well, when you start talking to me or someone else about this problem, you are now talking behind Coach 2's back. Listen to what The Message says in Proverbs 24:28–29—"Don't talk about your neighbors behind their backs—no slander or gossip, please. Don't say to anyone, 'I'll get back at you for what you did to me. I'll make you pay for what you did!'"

When you talk badly about Coach 2 behind her back, you're letting anger and being upset turn into the sin of gossip. And if I listen, I become an accomplice to your sin. Coach 2 hasn't had a chance to explain herself. I'm sure she didn't intend to make you angry, but she's never going to know she did unless you tell her.

Coach 1: I don't see how I can do that.

Visionary: Why not?

Coach 1: Well, it would feel awkward. I'd rather just let it go.

Visionary: Yes, it might be awkward at first, but the Bible says that talking directly to her is the only right thing to do. Otherwise, your hurt will turn to bitterness, and you'll fall into the sin trap of gossip.

Coach 1 (*begrudgingly and quietly*): Yes, I suppose you're right.

Visionary: As Christian leaders, we need to set an example of following the Bible's guidelines for confronting conflict. Even though someone talks about you behind your back, talking about the person doesn't make you any better. It's OK to be angry, but you need to try and work it out with the person before you tell others. And you know what?

Coach 1: What?

Visionary: I'm sure Coach 2 will appreciate your talking to her in person rather than talking to me and others, just like you wish she had done with you. Right?

Coach 1: Yes, but it really isn't that big a deal after all . . . I guess (*trying to squirm out of having to face Coach 2*).

Visionary (*understanding the reluctance, but not avoiding what needs to be done*): Oh, I think it is a big deal. It was big enough for you to call me. I tell you what, let's give you a week, and then I'll call you to be sure you've called Coach 2 and gone through the seven biblical steps to resolving conflict together. Then, when you talk to her, if you aren't satisfied with her response, the three of us can get together, and I'll be a mediator. Look back in Matthew 18:15–17. Jesus instructs us that including a third neutral person is your next recourse after talking in person. Let's pray about this right now.

(Bow heads and pray together.)

SKIT 2

Coach 1 and Coach 2 using the "7 Biblical Steps to Resolving Conflict."

STEP ONE

Coach 1 (*calling on the phone.*)

Coach 2 (*picks up the phone*): Hello?

Coach 1: Hello, Coach 1, this is Coach 2. I was wondering if we could get together for a cup of coffee. There are some things I'd like to discuss with you.

Coach 2: Oh, really? What are they? Can't we just talk about them on the phone?

Coach 1: No, I'd really like to meet with you. Could we meet for coffee Saturday morning say at 9:00? I'll even buy.

Coach 2: Well, I can't turn that down. OK. That should work. I'll see you then.

(*Both say good-bye and hang up.*)

STEP TWO

Coach 1 and Coach 2 sitting across from each other at a table at coffee shop sipping coffee.

Coach 1: Coach 2, you know how much I value you as a person and I really enjoy doing ministry with you, but I'd like to talk about a couple things. First, can we agree that we both want the common best for the ministry and our friendship?

Coach 2: Sure. I like working with you, too, and you do a great job as a shepherd coach.

Coach 1: Let's pray then before we get started.

Coach 2: Yeah. OK.

Coach 1: Lord, we thank You for our friendship and allowing us to work together. We know that You don't want anything coming between us as fellow team members and friends. Help us resolve any issues we might have with each other and please guard our tongues and minds. In Jesus' name we pray, amen.

Coach 2: Amen.

Coach 1: Well, the reason I wanted to meet with you is to ask if you've been saying that I spend money foolishly?

STEP 3
Coach 2 (*squirming in her seat*): Well, I didn't say you spend money foolishly. I just said you always seem to have money to burn and you've been buying a lot of new things lately when the rest of us are just scraping by. I didn't mean anything by it. It was just a passing comment. I just wondered how you do it. I don't know why this should bother you. I wasn't attacking your character. I was just

commenting on how lucky you are to be able to go places and have nice things. Who told you I said that anyway?

Step 4

Coach 1: Thank you for being honest. I can appreciate that it might have seemed like a casual comment to you, but can I tell you how it seemed to me?

Coach 2: Sure.

Step 5

Coach 1: I don't believe that you intentionally set out to bad-mouth me, but I hope you can see that it came across that way to me. It seemed as if you were questioning how I made my money, and that I wasn't using it wisely. And the worst part was that you were saying all of this behind my back. It made me wonder what other things you might be saying, and why do you care how I spend my money?

I do work hard and God has blessed me. Our family faithfully tithes and I serve in ministry. We have many areas where we donate, but there's also enough left over for us to enjoy. I don't think I flaunt my money, nor do I use it as an excuse not to serve. Do you see me doing that?

Step 6

Coach 2: No, I don't, and I'm sorry if I offended you. It certainly wasn't my intention. You're right; it isn't my business how you spend your money, and I was out of line talking about it to others. Maybe I'm jealous. I wish I could do the things for my family that you do.

STEP 7

Coach 1: You could. Maybe one of these days you and I could get together and I could show you how to set up a budget and share with you some of the ways we determine how to spend our money. That's really all we did in the beginning, and that allowed us to make some good investments and there was enough left over for us to enjoy. We really don't make that much money, but we do try to follow some specific guidelines for saving and spending.

Coach 2: I've never had a budget. We just earn it and spend it and earn it and spend more than we earn.

Coach 1: We used to be like that, too. Thank you for meeting with me today so we could get this settled. I have to tell you that I almost gossiped myself because I first went to our visionary director with my concerns, but she referred me to the seven biblical steps to resolving conflict that our team committed to abide by in the Team Conflict-Resolution Covenant. And look . . . it works!

Coach 2: It sure does! In the future, I'm only going to talk about myself.

Coach 1: Me too. And I'm also going to go directly to the person I have a problem with, or I think has a problem with me, and not talk to others first.

Coach 2: So how about a refill on our coffee? Are you still buying?

(*Both laugh and get up to get more coffee.*)

SKIT 3

Same scenario but Coach 2 refuses to meet with Coach 1, requiring the visionary director to intervene as a mediator.

Coach 1 (*calling on the phone.*)

Coach 2 (*picks up the phone*): Hello?

Coach 1: Hello, Coach 2, this is Coach 1. I was wondering if we could get together for a cup of coffee. There are some things I would like to discuss with you.

Coach 2: Oh, really? What are they? Can't we just talk about them on the phone?

Coach 1: No, I would really like to meet with you. Could we meet for coffee Saturday morning, say at 9:00? I'll even buy.

Coach 2: I'm sorry. I don't have time to meet with you. If you can't tell me what the problem is on the phone, then it must not be that bad. So is there anything else you want to talk about?

Coach 1: I need to meet with you in person, and if you're not willing to do that, I'm going to ask our visionary director to intervene as a mediator.

Coach 2: Suit yourself. Good-bye.

Coach 1: Good-bye.

Coach 1 (*calling on phone.*)

Visionary: Hello.

Coach 1: Hello. This is Coach 1. I did what you said to do and called Coach 2, but she wouldn't meet with me. She wanted to talk on the phone so I told her that I was going to ask you to mediate.

Visionary: I'm sorry to hear that. I'll call Coach 2 and arrange for the three of us to meet.

SCENE: THE THREE-WAY MEETING WITH ALL SEATED AT A TABLE.

STEP 1

Visionary: Let's pray. Lord, we pray that You will help us resolve the issues between these two valuable Coaches. Help us to hear each other and to come to a good conclusion. Let our speech be pleasant to you.

STEP 2

Visionary: You're both very valuable to the team, but you can't continue working effectively as long as there's a conflict between you. The Bible is very specific in Matthew 18:15–17 and Philippians 4:2–3 that if the two of you cannot resolve the issue on your own, than a third person needs to mediate. We need to remember that the work of the Lord is more important than our individual concerns, so I would like us to get the air cleared between the two of you right here. Coach 1 called me and wanted to talk about the situation, but I directed her to call you, Coach 2, and ask to meet with you as we all agreed in the Team Conflict-Resolution Covenant and the seven biblical steps to resolving conflict. Step 1 is to meet face-to-face. So here we are. I'm going to act as the mediator and ask Coach 1 to explain to you the issue that's bothering her.

Coach 1: Well, the reason I wanted to meet with you is to ask if you've been saying that I spend money foolishly?

Step 3

Coach 2 (*squirming in her seat*): Well, I didn't say you spend money foolishly. I just said you always seem to have money to burn and you've been buying a lot of new things lately when the rest of us are just scraping by. I didn't mean anything by it. It was just a passing comment. I just wondered how you do it. I don't know why this should bother you. I wasn't attacking your character. I was just commenting on how lucky you are to be able to go places and have nice things. Who told you I said that anyway?

Visionary: Let's just keep this between the two of you. Coach 1, what is your response to Coach 2?

Step 4

Coach 1: Thank you for being honest. I can appreciate that it might have seemed like a casual comment to you, but can I tell you how it seemed to me?

Coach 2: I think you're really overreacting. I didn't know that you were so sensitive!

Visionary: Coach 2, you just heard from Coach 1 that the things you said about her were offensive, and you've admitted to saying them. Let's see what Coach 1's response is to you.

STEP 5

Coach 1: I don't believe that you intentionally set out to bad-mouth me, but I hope you can see that it came across that way to me. It seemed as if you were questioning how I made my money, and that I wasn't using it wisely. And the worst part was that you were saying all of this behind my back. It made me wonder what other things you might be saying, and why do you care how I spend my money?

I do work hard and God has blessed me. Our family faithfully tithes and I serve in ministry. We have many areas where we donate, but there's also enough left over for us to enjoy. I don't think I flaunt my money, nor do I use it as an excuse not to serve. Do you see me doing that?

STEP 6

Coach 2: No, I don't, and I'm sorry if I offended you. It certainly wasn't my intention. You're right; it isn't my business how you spend your money, and I was out of line talking about it to others. Maybe I'm jealous. I wish I could do the things for my family that you do.

STEP 7

Coach 1: You could. Maybe one of these days you and I could get together and I could show you how to set up a budget and share with you some of the ways we determine how to spend our money.

That's really all we did in the beginning, and that allowed us to make some good investments and there was enough left over for us to enjoy. We really don't make that much money, but we do try to follow some specific guidelines for saving and spending.

Coach 2: I've never had a budget. We just earn it and spend it and earn it and spend more than we earn.

Coach 1: We used to be like that too. Thank you for meeting with me today so we could get this settled. I have to tell you that I almost gossiped myself because I first went to our visionary director with my concerns, but she referred me to the seven biblical steps to resolving conflict that our team committed to abide by in the Team Conflict-Resolution Covenant. And look . . . it works!

Coach 2: It sure does! In the future, I'm only going to talk about myself.

Coach 1: Me too. And I'm also going to go directly to the person I have a problem with, or I think has a problem with me, and not talk to others about it first.

Visionary: Now, that's what I like to hear. You just successfully worked through an issue in a biblical way and you can now help team members do the same. How about another cup of coffee?

(*All laugh and get up to get more coffee.*)

Case Study

A MINISTRY VISIONARY DIRECTOR'S SITUATION:

A member of my women's ministry team rarely came to meetings. When she did, she would volunteer for tasks and then wouldn't ever do them. I ended up doing all her work.

How would you deal with this situation?

THE MINISTRY VISIONARY DIRECTOR'S SOLUTION:

My advice would be to start by having a simple "Is everything all right?" kind of conversation and see where that leads. I finally called her to talk and said I sensed that her "heart just wasn't in women's ministry anymore." As it turned out, she and her husband had not been happy at our church and had been thinking about going back to their old church. So she stepped down from the team. It turned out well. I didn't feel like the "bad guy," and she made the decision.

What would you do if she didn't voluntarily step down?

THE MINISTRY VISIONARY DIRECTOR'S RESOLUTION:

I already had thought and prayed about my course of action if this particular woman had not resigned. Even though it would not have been easy, I first would have done whatever I could to talk kindly but firmly about the quality of her service with the goal of growth and restoration. Then, if that had not produced fruit, I would have asked her to step down until she felt she could return with a commitment to the team.

Journal

About His Work Ministries is Janet Thompson's writing and speaking ministry. Janet is about His work helping women realize the importance and value of relationships and God's call in Titus 2:1–5 to teach and train the next generation through mentoring and sharing life experiences. In 1996, Janet answered God's call to "Feed My sheep" by founding the Woman to Woman Mentoring Ministry at Saddleback Church in Lake Forest, California. Through her authored resources, Woman to Woman Mentoring: How to Start, Grow, and Maintain a Mentoring Ministry (LifeWay Press) and "Face-to-Face" Bible study series (New Hope Publishers), Janet has helped churches around the world start woman-to-woman mentoring in their own churches. In The Team That Jesus Built: How to Develop, Equip, and Commission a Women's Ministry Team, Janet shares the many team-building lessons she learned from Jesus.

FOR MORE INFORMATION AND TO CONTACT JANET:

Janet Thompson

About His Work Ministries — Conference and retreat speaking, mentoring, and coaching aspiring writers and ministry leaders

Two About His Work — Janet and her daughter Kim's conference and retreat speaking ministry

Email: info@womantowomanmentoring.com

www.womantowomanmentoring.com

Please share with Janet how you have used this book to build, remodel, or refurbish your team.

Also by **Janet Thompson**

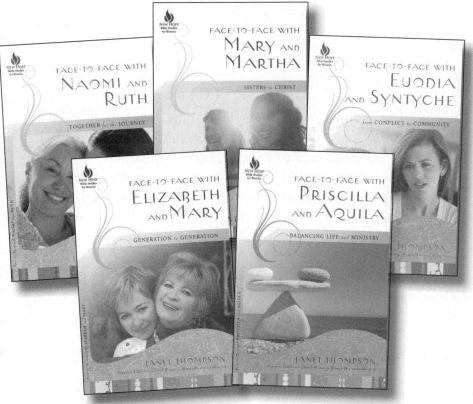

**Face-to-Face with
Naomi and Ruth**
Together for the Journey
ISBN-13: 978-1-59669-253-4

**Face-to-Face with
Euodia and Syntyche**
From Conflict to Community
ISBN-13: 978-1-59669-281-7

**Face-to-Face with
Mary and Martha**
Sisters in Christ
ISBN-13: 978-1-59669-254-1

**Face-to-Face with
Elizabeth and Mary**
Generation to Generation
ISBN-13: 978-1-59669-252-7

**Face-to-Face with
Pricilla and Aquila**
Balancing Life and Ministry
ISBN-13: 978-1-59669-295-4

Available in bookstores everywhere.

NEW HOPE
P U B L I S H E R S

For information about these books or any New Hope product, visit
www.newhopepublishers.com.

New Hope® Publishers is a division of WMU®, an international organization that challenges Christian believers to understand and be radically involved in God's mission.
For more information about WMU, go to www.wmu.com.
More information about New Hope books may be found at www.newhopepublishers.com. New Hope books may be purchased at your local bookstore.

Use the QR reader on your smartphone to visit us online at **www.newhopepublishers.com**

If you've been blessed by this book, we would like to hear your story. The publisher and author welcome your comments and suggestions at: newhopereader@wmu.org.